DRIVING STANDAR

GW00758629

DRIVING SKILLS

YOUR LARGE GOODS VEHICLE DRIVING TEST

**including the
Officially Recommended Syllabus**

London: **HMSO**

Technical Writer	Philip Martin, Driving Standards Agency
Graphics by	Vicky Squires

Published by HMSO

© Crown Copyright 1994

First Published 1994

ISBN 0 11 551192 X

Acknowledgements

The Driving Standards Agency would like to thank the members of staff of the following organisations for their contribution in the production of this publication

Army School of Mechanical Transport (Leconfield)
Department of Transport
Derbyshire Constabulary (Traffic Division)
DSA Driving Establishment (Cardington)
DVLA Swansea
Kent County Constabulary (Crime Prevention)
Maple Commercial Vehicle Security Systems
Motec (Telford)
T Knox Esq. (Formerly RTITB Training Officer KTT Group)
Nottingham Constabulary (Traffic Division)

The photograph on page 210 appears by kind permission of the Ross-Parry picture agency

The Large Goods Vehicle (LGV) Driver

As an LGV driver, **YOU** have a special responsibility - not just to yourself, but also to all other road users. A professional driver should set an example to other drivers by ensuring that the vehicle is driven, at all times, with the utmost safety and with courtesy and consideration for everyone else on today's busy roads.

To become a large goods vehicle driver you must not only possess a high degree of skill in the handling of your vehicle, but must also be prepared to make allowances for the behaviour of others. The right attitude and approach to your driving, together with a sound knowledge and the ability to apply defensive driving techniques are essential.

By successfully passing your car driving test, you have already shown that you reached the standard set for driving a motor vehicle unsupervised on today's roads. This book lists the skills which you must now master in order to pass the vocational driving test.

Put the information it contains into practice and you should be able to reach the higher standards demanded, go on to earn the privilege of driving large goods vehicles and above all, experience *'Safe driving for life'*

David E. Norris
Chief Driving Examiner
Driving Standards Agency

About this book

Your Large Goods Vehicle Driving Test
Has been written in four easy to read parts

Part 1 Before the LGV Driving Test

Because today's LGV driver needs to be thoroughly **professional** it is essential to appreciate the range of knowledge which the newcomer to driving large goods vehicles will need to acquire.

All this is in addition to the driving skills which need to be learned in order to drive lorries safely and competently.

The first section takes the new driver through applying for a provisional LGV licence, and includes details of current medical requirements.

The section goes on to cover aspects of driver awareness of the differences between driving lorries and cars. Forces at work on the vehicle and its load are also explained.

The importance of driver attitudes, different vehicle characteristics, together with an outline of weight, length, and – in particular – height restrictions applying to LGVs are all explained in the established DSA easy to read style.

Part 2 The Large Goods Vehicle Driving Test

Applying for the test and the content of the actual test itself are described fully in sections 8 and 9.

Part 3 Driving LGVs

Defensive driving, as well as driving in various weather conditions, at night, on motorways, dealing with accidents and emergencies are all covered in sections 10 to 14.

Part 4 Additional Information

DSA Service Standards and Citizens' Charter information, lists of Regional Offices, LGV driving test centres, useful addresses are all included in this section – together with licence category details, traffic signs etc.

Contents

Part 1 Before Applying for The LGV Driving Test

Contd. ▶

Contents

Part 2 — The LGV Driving Test

Contd. ▶

Part 3 — Driving LGVs

Part 4 — Additional Information

THE DRIVING SKILLS SERIES

ISBN 0 11 551158 X

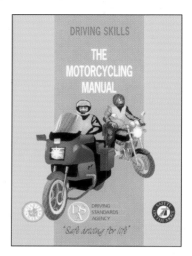

ISBN 0 11 550974 7

ISBN 0 11 551054 0

ISBN 0 11 551209 8

Coming soon

1. Applying for a provisional licence to drive LGVs

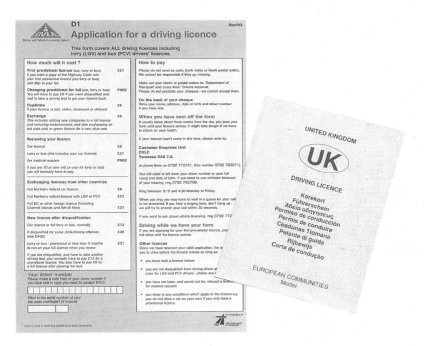

If you have not held a large goods vehicle licence before you must first apply to DVLC Swansea for the provisional entitlement to be added to your full motor car (Category B) licence. **You must not drive any large goods vehicle until you have received this entitlement**.

This section explains the requirements for being granted a licence to drive large goods vehicles.

Information about driving licences in general is set out in the Driver and Vehicle Licensing Agency leaflet D100 obtainable from Post Offices, Traffic Area Offices, Vehicle Registration Offices or by applying to Customer Enquiries Unit DVLC Swansea SA6 7JL.

Contents

Apply to

The Vocational Licence Section

Driver and Vehicle Licensing Centre (DVLC) Swansea SA99 1BR

Enclosing the following documents:

- A completed application form (D1)
- Your full motor car driving licence (Category **B**, previously Group A)

or

Your provisional motor car driving licence and test pass certificate* (D10)

- A completed Medical Report form (D4) signed by a doctor

• The appropriate fee

– Cheque

or

– Postal Order

(Made payable to 'Department of Transport' and crossed 'Drivers Account')

Do not send

cash

banknotes

blank postal orders

Write your

– name
– address
– date of birth
– driver number if you have one

on the back of your cheque.

Application Form *D1* (Rev/93)

You can obtain Form D1 from

– Post Offices

– Traffic Area Offices

– Vehicle Registration Offices (VROs)

or

Customer Enquiries Unit DVLC Swansea SA6 7JL

Make sure you fill in the form correctly (tear off the notes page and only return the form itself).

Everyone must fill in the green parts of the form.

Lorry and bus drivers must fill in the blue parts as well.

*This must be exchanged within two years of passing your test.

Note: Post-dated cheques cannot be accepted.

Note: the eyesight requirements are much more stringent than the motor car licence eyesight standards.

The LGV Learner Driver

In order to drive an LGV you must

- Be 21 yrs of age or over, unless you are a member of the armed forces on duties authorised by the Ministry of Defence

- Have a FULL* driving licence entitlement for Category **B** vehicles.

  This licence currently gives the automatic entitlement to Sub Category C1+E (Light Goods 3.5–7.5T gross) [plus a trailer not exceeding 750Kgs 7.5T+750Kg=8.25T Max].

- Hold

either
A full LGV licence for the category of vehicle being driven

  (Either Cat C or C+E)

  Drivers who hold an existing Class 2 or 3 (HGV) licence and who wish to drive articulated LGVs will need to take the LGV driving test to obtain **full** C+E entitlement

or
  A provisional LGV driving licence entitlement

- Meet the eyesight and medical requirements (see Section 2.)

Provisional LGV licence

If you are the holder of a provisional LGV licence entitlement

You must

- Only drive under the supervision of a person over 21 yrs who holds a full UK LGV licence for the category of vehicle being driven

- Display L-plates to the front and rear of the vehicle.

Vehicles with automatic transmission

If you take the LGV driving test in a vehicle with automatic transmission your full LGV driving licence will restrict you to driving only LGVs fitted with automatic transmission.

Only if the vehicle does not have a clutch pedal is it classified as an 'automatic'.

* **Note:** Candidates are no longer able to hold a provisional Category B licence while driving an LGV — removing the former 'dual test' facility.

Note: Many modern vehicles have transmission systems where sensors select the next gear without the driver using the clutch pedal.

2. Medical Requirements

Because driving a large goods vehicle carries a heavy responsibility to all other road users, it is vital that you meet exacting medical standards.

Your eyesight must meet much more stringent standards than that of ordinary drivers.

Remember, you may be refused a licence to drive large goods vehicles if you suffer from any serious medical condition which may cause road safety problems when driving lorries.

It is your responsibility to notify the DRIVERS MEDICAL UNIT at DVLC Swansea SA99 1TU immediately if you have, or develop, any serious illness or disability (likely to last more than three months) which could affect your driving.

Contents

Eyesight Requirements for LGV Drivers

All drivers, for whatever category of vehicle, must be able to read in good daylight a number plate at 20.5 metres (67 feet), and, if glasses or contact lenses are required to do so, these must be worn while driving.

In addition

i.   An applicant who has not held a goods vehicle or bus licence before must by law have both

• A visual acuity of at least 6/9 in the better eye.

and

• A visual acuity of at least 6/12 in the other eye.

He or she must also

• Have satisfactory uncorrected visual acuity.

Any applicant who has uncorrected acuity of less than 3/60 in both eyes will **not** be able to meet the required standard.

A driver who has an uncorrected acuity of less than 3/60 in one eye **may** be able to meet the required standard and should check with

Drivers Medical Unit
DVLC
Swansea SA99 1TU

ii.   An applicant or licence holder who has held an LGV/PCV (formerly HGV/PSV) licence before 1-3-92 but who does not meet the standard in (i) above **may** still qualify for a licence. Information about the standard for such an applicant can be obtained from DRIVERS MEDICAL UNIT, (address above).

Where medical considerations include a relevant date DVLC will make enquiries to establish the licensing position of all applicants at the date(s) in question.

An applicant or licence holder failing to meet the epilepsy, diabetes or eyesight regulations must be refused in law.

[If you are restricted to eyesight in one eye only you must declare this on Form D1]

Your qualified practitioner will use the Snellens test card to determine your eyesight standard.

Medical Examination and Form D4

(Previously DTp20003)

If this is your first application for LGV entitlement this medical report must be completed by a doctor.

You will also need to send one if you are renewing your LGV(HGV) licence and you are aged 45 or over unless you have already sent one during the last 12 months. You will need to have a medical examination in order to complete Form D4.

Consult your doctor first if you have any doubts about your fitness.

Only complete the applicant details and declaration on page 6 (Section 8) when you are with your doctor at the time of the examination.

This report is **not** available free under the National Health rules.

Your doctor is entitled to charge the current fee for this medical.

You are responsible for payment of this fee.

It cannot be recovered from DVLC.

The fee is not refundable if your application is refused.

The completed form must be received by DVLC within four months of the date of your doctor's signature.

Study the notes on pages 1 and 2 (remove these two pages before sending in your application)

Your doctor will complete Sections 1 to 7

Section 1 Vision

Please see eyesight notes on previous page

Section 2 Nervous System

Section 3 Diabetes Mellitus

Section 4 Psychiatric Illness

Section 5 General

Section 6 Cardiac

Section 7 Medical Practitioner Details

Medical Standards

You may be refused an LGV driving licence if you suffer from any of the following

- Liability to Epilepsy/ Seizure
- Diabetes requiring insulin (unless you held a licence on 1.4.91 and the Traffic Commissioner who issued that licence had knowledge of your condition)
- Visual defects (see eyesight requirements above)
- Heart disorders
- Persistent high blood pressure (see notes for details)
- Strokes/unconscious lapses within the last 5 years
- Any disorder causing vertigo within the last 2 years
- Severe head injury with serious continuing after effects, or major brain surgery
- Parkinson's disease, multiple sclerosis or other 'chronic' nervous disorders likely to affect the use of the limbs
- Mental disorders
- Alcohol/drug problems
- Serious difficulty in communicating by telephone in an emergency
- Visual field defects.

3. The LGV Driver

Driving a large goods vehicle requires skill combined with the right attitude and application of sound defensive driving techniques.

From the start, you need to appreciate the differences between driving smaller vehicles and driving large goods vehicles.

It is essential to understand the laws which relate to the forces at work on your vehicle and its load.

This section is about keeping control of your vehicle at all times.

Contents

Professional Standards

The road transport industry is subject to an extremely large number of regulations and requirements relating to

– drivers

– operators

– companies

– vehicles

– goods

– workshops.

To become a **professional** large goods vehicle driver you will need

• The demanding driving skills required

• The knowledge to deal with all the regulations which apply to your work

• A comprehensive knowledge of The Highway Code, including the meaning of traffic signs and road markings (especially ones which indicate a restriction for large goods vehicles).

The first, and most important, thing to learn is that the way you drive is vitally important.

• Drive properly and the goods entrusted into your care will arrive safely at their destination

• Drive dangerously or even carelessly and the potential for disaster is enormous.

From the start, recognise that whether you are driving an unladen lorry at the 7.5 tonnes end of the scale, or a fully laden articulated vehicle in the order of 38 tonnes or more, you can never act hastily without serious consequences resulting.

A loaded LGV travelling at speed and colliding with a stationary car (waiting to turn right, or held up on the motorway for example) will, in the majority of cases, reduce that car to scrap metal.

The graphic pictures on television and in the newspapers following a serious multi-vehicle motorway pile up are testimony to this.

You are the one with the responsibility of driving **your** vehicle safely at all times.

Your LGV licence is a privilege which requires effort to gain, and even more effort to keep.

Give some thought to the fact that many modern vehicles have the owners' details — name, address etc. on display.

How easy it is for others to report instances of bad driving.

How much better to set good examples of skill, courtesy and tolerance to other road users.

If you drive a smart, distinctive, well-maintained vehicle, make sure your driving matches the same high standards.

Be a credit to yourself, your company and your profession.

Becoming an LGV driver

Study the information in Section 6 which deals with vehicle characteristics.

You will need to understand how various kinds of large goods vehicles handle in order to drive them safely.

From car to lorry

To drive a lorry safely you must first appreciate the main differences between driving larger vehicles and driving smaller ones.

These are

- Weight
- Width
- Length
- Height
- Distance needed to pull up
- Distance needed to overtake

- Control needed when going downhill
- Power needed to climb uphill
- The need to avoid any sudden changes of speed or direction.

Some of these aspects will be obvious from the moment you first start to drive a large goods vehicle.

Other features will only become apparent after you have started to drive one.

The essential factor is to recognise that much more forward planning is needed to drive a lorry **safely.**

From Rigid to Articulated vehicles

You may already have experience of driving a rigid vehicle. (Formerly Heavy Goods Vehicle Groups [HGV]2 and 3)

The information in this book about driving articulated vehicles and rigid vehicle plus trailer combinations is to help you prepare for the LGV driving test to obtain Category **C + E** entitlement.

If you have already driven a rigid lorry towing a trailer (other than small compressors, etc.) this book will help you to prepare for the LGV driving test in order to obtain full **(unrestricted) C + E** entitlement.

Understanding LGVs

The first thing any LGV driver **must** understand is the effect the forces acting on the vehicle will have.

A basic law of physics states that every body will remain at rest or travel at a constant speed in a straight line unless acted upon by an external force.

This section looks at the effects of various forces on the vehicle and its load.

When a vehicle accelerates, brakes or changes direction forces are applied to it and its load.

The more violent or sudden the change the greater the forces.

An LGV

– laden or unladen

– rigid vehicle

– towing a drawbar trailer

– articulated vehicle

travelling in a straight line under gentle acceleration **is stable.**

Sudden

- **Steering**
- **Acceleration**
- **Braking**

can introduce forces which can cause severe loss of control.

All braking must be carried out smoothly and in good time.

Hydraulic braking systems

If you find you need to 'pump' the brakes STOP as safely as you can in a convenient place and check for any leaks in the hydraulic system.

Do not drive on unless you are sure you can stop safely.

Forces at work on your vehicle

The purpose of most LGVs is to carry goods.

Before looking at loading and load restraint in more detail, it is essential that you understand the effects of forces acting on your vehicle.

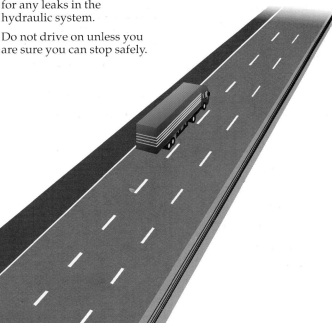

Friction

This is the grip between two surfaces.

The grip which the rubber tyres have on the road surface produces the traction (force) which is essential when

- moving away or accelerating
- turning/changing direction
- braking/slowing down.

The amount of traction will depend on

- The weight of the vehicle
- The vehicle's speed
- The condition of the tyre tread
- How the tyre is inflated
  - correct pressure
  - under
  - over
- The type and condition of the road surface
  - anti-skid
  - loose
  - smooth
- Weather conditions
  - fine and dry
  - rain
  - ice
  - snow

- Any other material present
  - mud
  - wet leaves
  - diesel spillage
  - other slippery spillages
  - inset metal rail lines
- The rate of change of speed or direction (sudden steering/braking)
- Condition of mechanical components
  - steering alignment
  - suspension.

Sudden acceleration or deceleration introduces additional forces on the vehicle which can overcome the friction of the tyre tread on the road surface.

Under these conditions the vehicle will

- lose traction (wheelspin)
- break away on a turn (skid)
- not stop safely (skid)
- overturn.

Jack-knifing

In the case of an articulated vehicle, severe braking can result in 'jack-knifing' as the tractive unit is pushed by the semi-trailer pivoting around the coupling (fifth wheel).

This is even more likely if the vehicle was not travelling in a straight line when the brakes were applied.

Similar results will occur with a drawbar trailer — where there may be TWO pivoting points

– at the coupling pin

– and at the turntable of the front wheels of a two or more axle trailer.

Changing into a lower gear when travelling at too high a speed, or releasing the clutch suddenly will produce much the same effect, since the braking effect will only be applied to the driven wheels.

Jack-knifing is usually more likely to occur with an unladen vehicle.

Trailer swing

Trailer swing can occur on a drawbar combination (or occasionally on an articulated vehicle) when

• Sharp braking is applied on a bend

• Excessive steering takes place at speed

• The brakes on either the tractive unit or trailer are not properly adjusted.

It follows that all braking, gear changes, steering and acceleration should be smooth and under full control.

Anti-jack knifing devices

For some years now, well-proven systems have been available which reduce the risk of jack-knifing on articulated vehicles.

Note: On vehicles equipped with retarders, a sophisticated system of electronic signals ensures that appropriate braking effort is applied to the trailer wheels.

Forces affecting your vehicle

Acceleration

Sudden and excessive power applied to the wheels causing the vehicle to accelerate **rapidly**, may cause the load to fall off the back of the vehicle.

Deceleration

If harsh braking forces are applied to the wheels

– the load may attempt to continue moving forward

– the tyres may lose their grip on the road surface causing the vehicle to skid

– the weight of the vehicle is transferred to the front axle, causing the front of the vehicle to 'dip' downward.

Sudden or violent steering

Any sudden steering movement may cause the load to attempt to continue in a straight line and fall off the vehicle.

Any movement of the load is likely to cause the vehicle to become unstable.

All acceleration and braking should be controlled and as smooth and progressive as possible.

Gravity

When a vehicle is stationary on level ground the only force generally acting upon it is the downward pull of gravity (ignoring wind forces etc.).

• On an uphill gradient

Gravity will have a greater effect on a moving vehicle and its load so that

– more power is needed from the engine to move the vehicle and its load forward and upward

– less braking effort is needed and the vehicle will pull up in a shorter distance.

• On a downhill gradient

The effects of gravity will tend to

– make the vehicle's speed increase

– require more braking effort

– increase stopping distances.

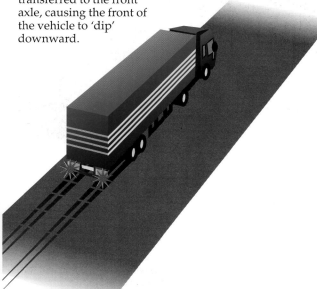

Centre of Gravity

The vehicle's centre of gravity is the point around which all of its weight is balanced.

To keep the vehicle and its load stable, this should be arranged to be

– as low as possible

– along a line running centrally down the length of the LGV.

The higher this centre of gravity occurs, the less stable the vehicle and/or its load will be.

As a result, the vehicle will become more easily affected by

– braking

– steering

– the slope (camber) of a road

– the wheels running over a kerb

and result in either the load tilting, falling off or the vehicle overturning.

Side Tipping Vehicles

Always select the firmest level site available before tilting the vehicle body.

Until the load is discharged all the weight will be transferred to one side.

Unless the vehicle is on firm level ground there is a risk of overturning.

End Tipper vehicles

When a loaded tipper vehicle body (whether tanker, bulk carrier, or high sided open body) is raised to discharge the load, the Centre of Gravity is raised to a critical position.

It is vitally important to ensure the vehicle is on a level, solid surface before engaging the hoist mechanism.

Refuse or construction sites

Particular care must be taken at waste disposal* or construction sites where the surface is often soft and uneven.

You should always resist any instruction to 'Tip it over there!' until *you* are sure it will be safe to do so.

* At least one site operator has banned the use of articulated tipper vehicles at its waste disposal sites because of instances of such vehicles overturning.

Kinetic Energy

This is the energy contained in a moving vehicle.

The amount depends on

– the mass (weight) of the vehicle + load

– the speed.

This energy must be reduced by the brakes in order to stop the vehicle.

The kinetic energy of a stationary vehicle is zero.

An increase in speed from 15 MPH to 45 MPH(x 3)

increases the kinetic energy

NINEFOLD (= 3 x 3)

If you reduce the speed by ½ from 50 MPH to 25 MPH the Kinetic Energy acting on your vehicle is ONE QUARTER of what it was before braking.

As the brakes reduce the speed of a vehicle, the kinetic energy is converted into heat.

Continuous use of the brakes can result in their becoming over-heated and losing their effectiveness (especially on long downhill gradients).

This is known as *brake fade*.

ALWAYS REMEMBER

The effort required to stop a fully laden LGV travelling at 56 MPH is so much greater than that needed to stop an ordinary motor car travelling at similar speed.

Added to this is the knowledge that you need to avoid harsh braking at all times when driving a LGV.

Momentum

This is the tendency for a vehicle and/or its load to continue in a straight line.

It depends on

– the mass (or weight)

– the speed.

The higher the speed the greater the momentum and the greater the effort required to

– stop

– change direction.

Forces acting on the load

If the forces acting on a load cause it to become detached from the vehicle, it will move in the direction of the force

• While accelerating

  – fall off the back

• While braking

  – continue moving forward

• While tilting

  – topple over

• While turning

  – continue on original path and fall off the side.

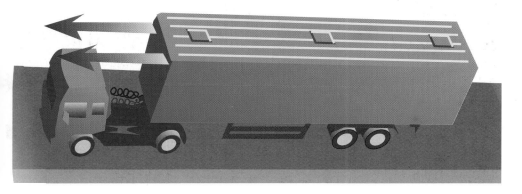

Centrifugal force

When the vehicle takes a curved path at a bend the forces acting upon the vehicle cause the vehicle to tend to continue on the original straight course.

At other than high speeds this force will be overcome by the traction of the tyres on the road surface.

If a loaded vehicle takes a bend at too high a speed the centrifugal force acting on the vehicle may cause the load to become detached and fall off the side or the vehicle to overturn.

Loss of Control

If you ask too much of your tyres, such as by turning **and** braking at the same time, you are dividing the available traction.

Once any or all the tyres lift, or slide **YOU**, the driver, are no longer in control of the vehicle.

Whatever forces are acting upon the vehicle will determine what happens next!

Vehicle and Load

When any change is made to the vehicle's motion or direction, *the same forces will act on any load being carried.*

Unless the load is secured to the vehicle so that it cannot move, and the traction between the tyres and the road surface is maintained — **YOU** WILL LOSE CONTROL OF YOUR VEHICLE.

Keeping control of your vehicle

Remember:

You cannot alter the severity of a bend

You cannot change the weight of the load

But *you do have control over the speed of your vehicle!*

To keep control

- Ensure all braking is
  - controlled
  - in good time
  - made when travelling in a straight line wherever possible
- Reduce speed BEFORE negotiating
  - bends
  - roundabouts
  - corners

- Avoid braking and turning at the same time (unless manoeuvring at low speed) – reduce speed first
- Look well ahead to assess and plan.

The forces described will always act on a vehicle in motion.

If you disregard them — you will probably lose control.

Allow for them in your driving.

The aftermath of a serious incident involving a large goods vehicle.

4. Driver attitudes

Open upon a time there used to be 'Knights of the Road' . . .

The public's image of the average lorry driver varies from that of a skilful saint manoeuvring what appears to be an enormous vehicle into almost impossible spaces — to that of an aggressive Demon-like figure intent on crushing every other road user beneath his monster truck.

It is for YOU as a new LGV driver to create the best possible image by setting good examples of driving for other drivers to follow.

Contents

Driver Attitudes

'Tailgating'

One of the most frequent criticisms levelled at LGV drivers is that other road users feel intimidated by large goods vehicles.

The sheer size, noise and appearance of a typical LGV often appears somewhat intimidating to a cyclist, pedestrian, or even the average car driver.

However, it is when an LGV appears to be driven in an aggressive way that other road users feel really threatened.

The most frequently quoted situation occurs when an LGV has travelled **dangerously** close behind a smaller vehicle, at speed, with only a few feet between them (usually in the second lane of a motorway).

In an effort to improve the image of the transport industry as a whole, some large retail organisations are reviewing the placing of contracts with any distributor whose vehicles have repeatedly been seen tailgating on motorways etc.

Police forces are so concerned at the number of accidents which have been caused as a direct result of vehicles driving much too close to the vehicle in front, that a number have mounted campaigns to video and prosecute offenders.

Tailgating and driving in close convoy with other LGVs are not only bad driving habits, but frequently have serious consequences.

Your view of the road ahead is seriously restricted and you are left with an impossible stopping distance.

Do not engage in this dangerous practice!

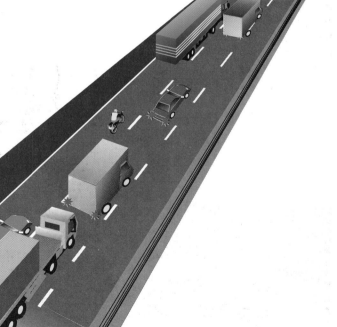

Speed

You can never justify driving too fast simply because you need to reach a given location by a specific time, whether it be a ferry, loading bay or depot.

If an accident results and you injure someone, or worse, there is no possible defence for your actions.

The introduction of 'Just in Time' flow-line policies reduces the need for manufacturers to hold large stocks of materials.

It is also intended to ensure fresh foods at the supermarket for example.

It must not place additional pressures on the driver!

Intimidation

Never allow yourself to get into the situation where you are using the size, weight and power of your vehicle to intimidate other road users.

Even the repeated 'hiss' from air brakes being applied or released while stationary gives the impression of 'breathing down the neck' of the driver in front.

Retaliation

You must at all times resist impatience or the temptation to retaliate in order to 'teach someone a lesson'.

Always drive

- Courteously
- With anticipation
- Allowing for other road users' mistakes
- With **full** control of your vehicle.

Remember:

When driving an LGV, you cannot act hastily without the possibility of serious loss of control.

Effects of your vehicle

You must recognise the effects of turbulence or 'buffeting' caused by your vehicle especially when overtaking

- pedestrians
- horse riders
- cyclists
- motorcyclists
- cars towing caravans
- cars
- other lorries and buses.

If you drive a maximum-length articulated LGV a similar effect occurs when smaller, lighter vehicles overtake at speed, especially on motorways.

As a competent LGV driver, you must always be aware of the effect your vehicle and your driving has on other road users.

On congested built-up roads, particularly in shopping areas, take extra care when you need to drive closer to the kerb.

Be aware of

- the possibility of a pedestrian stepping off the kerb (and under the rear wheels)
- the nearside mirror striking the head of a pedestrian standing at the edge of the kerb
- cyclists moving up on the nearside of your vehicle in slow-moving traffic.

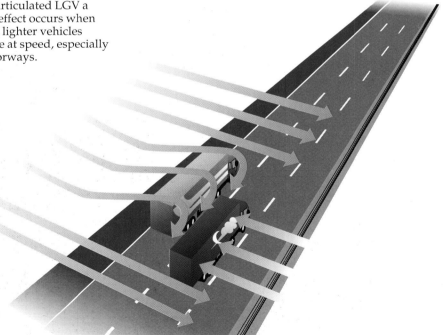

Use of the horn

Because LGVs are often equipped with powerful multi-tone air horns, their use should be strictly confined to the guidance set out in The Highway Code — to warn other road users of your presence.

Never use the horn aggressively.

Do not use the horn between 23.30 hrs and 07.00 hrs in a built-up area unless a moving vehicle poses a danger.

Use of the headlights

To avoid dazzle do not switch the headlights on to full beam when following another vehicle.

Do not switch on additional auxiliary lights which may be fitted to your vehicle unless weather conditions permit.

Never repeatedly flash the headlights while driving *directly behind* another vehicle.

Remember:

There is only one **official** use of 'flashing' the headlights described in The Highway Code –

that is to let other road users know you are there.

Be aware that by using any unauthorised 'code' of headlight flashing, you may be misunderstood by others — which in turn could lead to accidents.

Neither the horn(s) nor the headlights must be used to rebuke or to intimidate another road user.

Courtesy and consideration are the hallmarks of a professional driver.

5. Driver knowledge

This book will help you to

- Drive to the higher standards required
- Prepare for, and pass, the LGV driving test
- Be aware of the importance of driver attitude
- Take pride in your driving.

Use it throughout your preparation for the LGV driving test.

Contents

Basic knowledge

The first things you will need to know about your vehicle are its

– weight (restrictions)

– height (clearances etc.)

– width (restrictions)

– length (lay-bys, corners)

– ground clearance (low loader or dual purpose trailers only).

You will also need to know the speed limits which apply to your vehicle and the speed at which it will normally travel*.

Weight limits

Because this is an area where many offences occur, it is essential that, as a responsible driver, you are aware of, and understand, the limits relating to any vehicle you drive.

(For definitions of terms relating to weight limits, see the Glossary of Terms in Part 4)

Remember that weight limits in many cases refer to the maximum gross weight.

Certain increases in the permitted gross weight of vehicles engaged in 'inter-modal' operations between road and rail terminals are subject to a number of conditions

– the number of axles

– tyre specifications

– axle spacings

– road friendly suspension

(Special documentation is required to cover such movements between rail-head and road depot).

Road-friendly suspension

generally means that an axle is fitted with air suspension, or a suspension regarded as being equivalent to air suspension (by EC directive 92/7/EEC).

At least 75% of the spring effect is caused by an air spring (i.e. operated by air or some compressible fluid).

If this sounds complicated, it is intended to illustrate that the law relating to weight limits is complex.

Accurate information is required to ensure that not only does the vehicle comply with the law, but also that the driver is not committing any offence.

It is essential that **all** limits are complied with in order to avoid overloading and possible prosecution.

New technology allows local authorities to make spot weight checks on vehicles, identify them and inform the police who may escort them to the nearest official weighbridge.

* See page 34 for more detailed information relating to the movement of oversize loads — including use of marker boards, escort requirements, special movement order notices etc.

Weight Limits

Weight restrictions normally apply to the PLATED WEIGHT of a vehicle. Therefore, when tractive units of articulated LGVs are being driven without a trailer they are still subject to weight limits which relate to

– lighting regulations

– roads subject to weight limits

– lanes from which LGVs are banned on multi-lane motorways.

Regulations also include axle weight limits applying to the tractive unit which must not be exceeded when the vehicle is loaded.

It is essential that you, as the driver, ensure that the load is distributed correctly and safely either on, or in, your vehicle.

Generally, this means that loads are built up against the headboard or front wall of the body in order to reduce movement in transit.

Care must be taken to ensure that the *front* axle(s) of your vehicle are not overloaded.

Articulated vehicles and part-loads

To increase stability and reduce the risk of the trailer wheels lifting when turning, it is preferable to have part loads (such as an empty single ISO* container) located over the rear axle(s).

Whatever goods vehicle you drive, you should study the

Department of Transport Publication:

Code of Practice **SAFETY OF LOADS ON VEHICLES (HMSO)**

Recovery vehicles

Always make sure axle loading limits are not exceeded when a recovery vehicle removes another LGV by means of a suspended tow (sometimes overlooked).

Roadside checks frequently reveal contraventions of many weight limit regulations.

* International Standards Organisation.

Height Limits

Proposals for new height regulations to apply from 1994

Height

If you are the driver of any vehicle where the overall travelling height of the vehicle, its equipment and load (including any trailer)

is more than 3 metres (10 feet)

you should ensure that

- The overall travelling height of the vehicle, its equipment and load (including any trailer) is **conspicuously marked in figures not less than 40mm high**

  in such a manner that it can be read by the driver when in the driving position

  i. In feet + inches

  or

  ii. In feet + inches and a height in metres

- There is no more than 50mm difference between the height specified in feet + inches and the height specified in metres

- Any height indicated is not less than the overall travelling height of the vehicle

- This is the **only** indication of the overall travelling height.

(This notice does not apply to a tipper vehicle being driven while unloading).

Warning devices on vehicles fitted with high level equipment

If a vehicle is fitted with high level equipment with a maximum height of more than **3 metres**

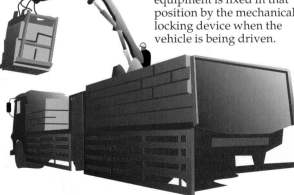

An audible and visual warning device should warn the driver if

- The height of the equipment exceeds the height shown on the sign in the cab or 3 metres in any other case

- The equipment is not in its designed travelling position.

- The equipment is between its designed maximum height and the height shown on the sign

  unless

  the equipment has a mechanical locking device which can lock the equipment in a stowed position and the equipment is fixed in that position by the mechanical locking device when the vehicle is being driven.

Important note: These proposals are still subject

Overhead clearances

Drivers of any vehicle exceeding 3 metres in height should exercise care when entering

– loading bays
– depots
– dock areas
– freight terminals
– service station forecourts
– any premises which have overhanging canopies

or negotiating

– bridges
– overhead cables
– overhead pipelines
– overhead walkways
– road tunnels.

Restrictions on use of high vehicles and loads

No vehicle or load with an overall travelling height exceeding

4.88 metres
should be moved by road unless the appropriate authorities have been given the required notice.

Overheight Loads

If the load exceeds

5.25 metres (17'6")

notification is required to be sent to telephone companies.

Electricity Supply Regulations 1988 state that the minimum height of electricity supply cables over roads must be at least 5.7m (19ft).

Any vehicle or load which exceeds

5.0 metres (16'6")

is at risk!

Contact the local Electricity Board for advice regarding advance notice required to be given to Electricity authorities concerned (at least 10 days) — including details of the load, routes etc. See your local telephone directory for details.

When planning the movement of such vehicles and loads, the Local Highways Authority will need to be contacted where overhead gantry traffic signs or suspended traffic lights are likely to be affected by loads over

5.7 metres (19ft)

to amendment at the time of publication

Part 1 Before the LGV Driving Test

Department of Transport and British Rail joint campaign to prevent 'Bridge Bashing'

Every year around EIGHT HUNDRED reported incidents occur involving vehicles or their loads hitting railway or motorway bridges. The actual number is now thought to be much higher.

Impact with any bridge can have serious consequences.

A Large Goods Vehicle or any part of its load colliding with a railway bridge could result in the bridge being weakened

The effect could be inconvenience to rail traffic at least, or the potential for a major disaster at worst. This is apart from the costs involved in making the bridge safe, re-aligning railway tracks and the general disruption to road and rail traffic.

Remember, the headroom under bridges in this country is at least 16'6" (5.0 m)

UNLESS OTHERWISE INDICATED

*In many instances this is **ONLY** between the limits marked where the overhead clearance is arched.*

If your vehicle collides with a bridge

Stop & Report

You must report the incident to the Police if a railway bridge is involved.

DO THIS IMMEDIATELY

to avoid a possible serious accident and loss of life.

OWN UP!

Never be tempted to 'Hit and Run'

Give information about

- The Location
- The Damage
- Any bridge reference number (often found on a plate bolted to the bridge or wall

BY LAW you are required to notify British Rail at the time.

You must also inform the Police within 24 hrs if you do not do so at the time of the incident.

Failure to do so is an offence.

You must know the height of your vehicle or its load

- Do not Guess
- Measure it!
- Do not Ignore
  - traffic signs
  - road markings
  - warning lights
- Pay attention!

Do not take chances.

Height guide

Feet	Metres
16' 6"	5.0
16	4.8
15	4.5
14	4.2
13	3.9
12	3.6
11	3.3
10	3.0
9	2.7

If you are not sure of the safe height STOP

Call British Rail, Works Group on **0345 581657** (all calls charged at local rate).

Remember

- Plan your route
- Slow down approaching bridges
- Know the overall vehicle/load height
- Keep to the centre of arched bridges
- Wait for a safe gap to proceed if there is oncoming traffic.

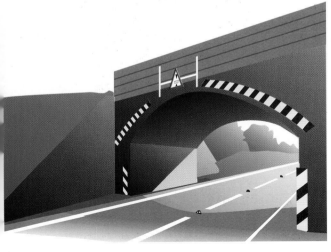

Width

As the driver of a **Large** goods vehicle, you must at all times be aware of the road space which the vehicle occupies.

This is particularly important where width is restricted — often because of parked or oncoming vehicles. The first casualty will probably be your offside or nearside mirror(s).

Not only can this cause injury to yourself and others, but it also renders your vehicle unroadworthy i.e. illegal.

Many local authorities are adopting 'traffic calming' measures and road width restrictions are becoming much more common.

Watch for them.

Overall width limits

2.75 m Locomotives
2.5 m   Motor tractors
2.5 m   Motor cars
2.5 m   Heavy motor cars
2.6 m   Refrigerated vehicles and trailers*
2.5 m   Trailers*
2.3 m   Other trailers

Wide loads

Loads projecting over **305mm**

Wide loads

2.9m to 3.5m

• Require side markers
• Police notification.

Wide loads

3.5m+ to 4.3m

• Require side markers
• Police notification
• An attendant.

Wide loads

4.3m+ to 5.0m

Require

• Side markers
• Police notification
• An attendant

and are subject to the following speed limits

30 MPH Motorways
25 MPH Dual carriageways
20 MPH All other roads

Wide loads between

5.0m to 6.1m

Require

• Side markers
• Police notification
• An attendant
• Department of Transport Approval

and are subject to the above speed limits.

The side marker boards must comply with regulations so that they show clearly on either side of the projection to the front and to the rear.

All marker boards must be independently lit at night time.

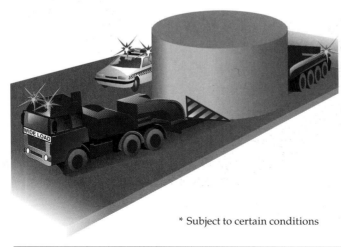

* Subject to certain conditions

Length

Locations where length restrictions apply are comparatively few

– road tunnels
– level crossings
– ferries

being the obvious ones.

However, drivers of long rigid vehicles — either with or without drawbar trailers, or articulated LGVs must be aware of the length of their vehicles especially when

– turning left or right
– negotiating roundabouts or mini roundabouts
– emerging from premises or exits
– overtaking
– parking, especially in lay-bys
– driving on narrow roads where there are passing places
– negotiating level crossings — see p 246 for detailed advice

Maximum length limit

12.0m	Rigid vehicles
16.5m	Articulated vehicles*
18.0m or 18.35m	Vehicle and trailer combinations**
18.0m	Articulated vehicles with low-loader semi-trailer (manufactured after 01-04-91) (not including step frame low loaders)

Car transporter semi trailers

12.5m	Kingpin to rear
4.19m	Kingpin to any point at the front

Other semi trailers

12m	Kingpin to the rear
2.04m	Kingpin to any point at the front
14.04m	Composite trailer
12m	Drawbar trailer with four or more wheels, and drawing vehicle is more than 3,500Kg MGW
7m	Other drawbar trailers

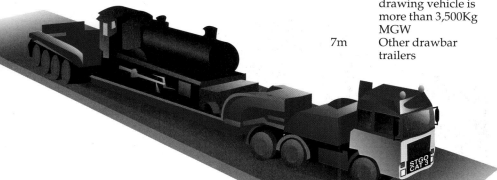

* Maximum length limit for vehicles designed to carry exceptionally long indivisible loads is 27.4m.

** See Construction & Use Regulations for details covering road trains.

Uncoupling and Re-coupling Articulated vehicles

Correct uncoupling sequence

1. Choose a safe level firm legal location
2. Stop the vehicle, apply the parking brake and stop the engine
3. Apply the trailer brake fully
4. Lower the landing gear (use supports if needed)
5. Stow the winding handle
6. Turn off any taps fitted to the air lines
7. Disconnect the air lines ('Suzies') and stow the lines safely
8. Disconnect the electric line and stow safely
9. Disconnect any 'dog-clip', securing the king-pin release handle
10. Release the fifth wheel coupling locking bar (if fitted)
11. Drive the tractive unit slowly forward OBSERVING the trailer landing
12. Take any anti-theft precautions (kingpin lock etc.)
13. Remove number plate, lenses, bulbs if theft or vandalism is likely to be a problem.

Uncoupling rigid vehicle plus trailer combinations

A similar sequence applies, except for the uncoupling of the trailer drawbar which will require supporting while the drawing vehicle moves away.

Correct Re-coupling sequence

1. Stop the tractive unit just ahead of, and lined up with, the trailer
2. Check the trailer parking brake is applied
3. Secure the unit and check coupling height and compatibility
4. Reverse the unit SLOWLY under the trailer until the kingpin mechanism is heard to lock into place
5. CHECK the coupling is secure by attempting to pull forward slightly, once or twice, against the trailer brake
6. Connect any king-pin release handle securing device ('dog-clip' etc.)
7. Connect the appropriate 'Suzie' air and electric lines and turn on any taps/valves, if fitted
8. Raise the landing gear and stow the handle securely
9. Release the trailer parking brake
10. Start up the engine and ensure gauges register correct pressures in air storage tanks and that no warning buzzer/light is operating
11. Obtain assistance to check for air line leaks and operation of all rear, marker, reversing lights, indicators, stop lights and fog light(s)
12. Secure the correct rear number plate and check all reflectors are present and clean
13. Examine all tyres, wheelnuts, fastenings, ropes, sheets, dropside locking clips, rear doors, hydraulic rams, tail lift gear etc. to ensure the trailer and any load will not present a danger to other road users
14. Check the function of any ABS* warning lights etc.
15. Make sure your mirrors are properly adjusted to give the best view down each side of the trailer before driving off.
16. Test the operation of the brakes at a safe place ideally BEFORE moving out on to a public road

Re-coupling rigid vehicle plus trailer combinations

The sequence is similar, but, the trailer drawbar will need to be adjusted to the correct height (often by means of a bottle jack) before the towing vehicle reverses to re-couple the trailer.

Be on the alert for the safety of anyone at the rear of your vehicle who is assisting you to re-couple the trailer.

*See p.39 Re: ABS.

Vehicle braking systems

It is vitally important that *you*, as the driver, understand the rules which apply to connecting and disconnecting the brake lines on either an articulated vehicle, or a rigid vehicle and trailer combination.

A three line system comprises – emergency RED line

– auxiliary BLUE line

– service YELLOW line

These must be connected *strictly* according to approved procedure.

Study the Department of Transport publication which gives instructions on vehicle braking systems and shows what is *acceptable* when connecting a 3 line drawing vehicle to a 2 line trailer (or vice versa).

- **HGV BRAKE SYSTEMS BRAKING CONNECTIONS FOR GOODS VEHICLES AND TRAILERS**

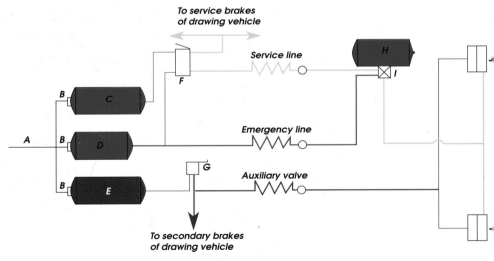

A – Supply from compressor	D – Service reservoir (Trailer)	G – Hand control valve
B – Non-return valves	E – Secondary reservoir	H – Trailer reservoir
C – Service reservoir (Vehicle)	F – Dual footvalve	I – Relay emergency valve
		J – Double diaphragm actuators

Example of ACCEPTABLE brake line connections: 3 line drawing vehicle – 3 line trailer

Vehicle Braking Systems

If taps (or hand-operated valves) are fitted, you must ensure they are opened after re-connecting, and closed before disconnecting brake lines.

Note: When coupling a motor vehicle fitted with automatic sealing valves in the 'Suzie' lines, ensure that the trailer is equipped to actuate them.

With some "spring brake" systems the brakes will be applied to the trailer when the emergency line is released.

On others the brakes will come off as air seeps away.

Before disconnecting any brake lines *Ensure that the trailer parking brake has been correctly applied.*

This precaution **MUST NOT** be overlooked!

There have been a number of fatal accidents which have been due to the trailer brakes 'lifting off' as the brake line is released — allowing the trailer to move.

Remember:

In cold frosty weather any water present in the air storage tanks may freeze and prevent pressure building up properly.

It is important to drain the reservoirs daily to remove moisture which has condensed as the air is drawn in by the compressor.

Some systems are self-venting.

Make sure you know which type is fitted to your vehicle.

Antilocking Braking Systems

(generally known as 'ABS')

Antilocking braking systems are required by law on certain large goods vehicle and trailer combinations.

The system simply means that sensors detect when the wheels are about to lock under braking.

The brakes are briefly released and then immediately re-applied — thus reducing the risk of skidding.

The presence of ABS does not, in any way, relieve the driver of the obligation to drive defensively, plan well ahead, and anticipate the need to brake smoothly and progressively.

Note: ABS is the Registered Trade Mark by BOSCH (Germany) for Anti Blockiersystem.

Care needs to be taken to ensure that the braking system on the tractive unit or rigid towing vehicle is compatible with the braking system on the semi-trailer or trailer.

Antilock braking system connections

Modern antilock braking systems require electrical power for their operation.

Multi-pin connectors are required to carry the electrical supply to operate the trailer brakes.

Vehicles with ABS must be identified by an ABS braking system fault warning indicator which is incorporated into the driver's console (for some combinations the trailer warning is on the trailer headboard).

The driver will need to know which vehicle combinations are required to have ABS fitted by law.

It is not only dangerous to drive a combination with the antilock braking system inoperative, it may also be illegal to do so.

Specialised knowledge

LGV drivers are subject to a wide variety of regulations.

It is essential that you keep up to date with all changes in road transport legislation which affect you.

Hazardous Goods Bulk or Packaged

Strict regulations regarding the stowage and labelling of materials classified as 'hazardous' must be observed.

Under the Road Traffic (Training of Drivers of Vehicles Carrying Dangerous Goods) Regulations 1992, known as the Driver Training Regulations (DTR), the operator of any vehicle used to carry dangerous goods must ensure that the driver of any such vehicle receives adequate instruction and training to enable them to understand

- Any emergency action which may be needed, and the dangers which may be created by the substances being carried

Note: 'Instruction' is the verbal and/or written information that must be given to a driver about their load(s) each day

Note: Existing qualifications under the 'Hazpak' training scheme will be valid until expiry of any current certificate, or 31st December 1994 — whichever is earlier.

- The driver's duties under the Health and Safety at Work Act 1974
- Any duty imposed by legislation which applies to carrying dangerous goods by road.

'Training' is the formal tuition of drivers to provide education about the hazards dangerous substances may present.

After 31 December 1994 the following groups of drivers will need to be in possession of a certificate showing that they are licensed by DVLC to carry dangerous goods by road.

- Drivers of road tankers with a capacity of more than 3000 litres, or a maximum permissible weight of over 3.5 tonnes

- Drivers of vehicles carrying tank containers, regardless of maximum permissible weight of the vehicle
- Drivers of all vehicles carrying explosives (subject to limited exemptions)
- Drivers of all vehicles over 3.5 tonnes maximum permissible weight which are subject to The Road Traffic (Carriage of Dangerous Substances in Packages,etc) Regulations 1992 [known as PGR].

This certificate will be valid for 5 years.

DVLC will only issue the certificate upon receipt of proof of attending a course at an approved training establishment *and* passing the 7357 examination of The City & Guilds of London Institute.

Petroleum and Compressed Gasses

The transport of inflammable materials is already the subject of stringent safety regulations and drivers of tanker vehicles carrying such materials must receive comprehensive specialist training relating to emergency procedures, loading, discharging*, fire precautions etc.

Waste Disposal

Drivers engaged in the transport of waste materials must comply with strict documentation procedures and be in possession of the necessary permits to move such materials to approved disposal sites.

The Carriage of Livestock

Drivers of livestock vehicles must comply with regulations which govern times, conditions (watering, temperature etc.) relating to the transport of livestock.

Vehicles used for this purpose may no longer be 'open-topped'.

Refrigerated Foodstuffs

Strict temperature controls need to be observed by drivers of refrigerated vehicles or trailer units.

During transit the rules governing these products must be followed.

Sophisticated monitoring equipment is widely used to ensure the requirements are being rigidly observed.

Skip Loaders

Whether the container is a small 'mini skip' type, or a larger bulk container skip, the skip body must be covered by a sheet or netting.

Any net must have a smaller mesh size than the pieces of material being carried to ensure the contents are not blown off, or do not fall on to the roadway.

Loose Materials

It is now a legal requirement that any loose materials such as sand, abrasive powders, grit etc. must be sheeted-over to prevent the contents flying into the air and causing a hazard to other road users.

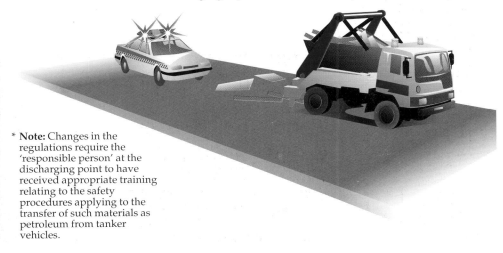

* **Note:** Changes in the regulations require the 'responsible person' at the discharging point to have received appropriate training relating to the safety procedures applying to the transfer of such materials as petroleum from tanker vehicles.

Load restraints

Securing the load

The information in this section has been known for many years as 'Roping & Sheeting'.

Changes in legislation mean that this covers many wider aspects.

When considering securing the load, a driver needs to take into account

– the nature of the load

– suitability of the vehicle

– stability of the load

– the type of restraint

– protection from weather

– prevention of theft

– ease of delivery.

The object is to ensure a secure load and a stable vehicle when

– braking

– steering

even in emergency situations.

The failure of tyres on the vehicle or trailer should not cause the load to become insecure.

This is particularly important when stowing loads such as wooden pallets, hay etc. which are usually stacked high on flat-bed vehicles.

It is, however, difficult to foresee the stresses placed on any vehicle or load in an accident situation.

Types of load

Simply because the load consists of large heavy pieces of machinery does not mean that it will stay in place throughout the journey.

Fatal accidents have occurred through such items falling from a vehicle, or shifting under braking or cornering.

When making a decision as to the type of restraints required consider what might happen if

- You have to brake hard **and** swerve to avoid an accident
- Your vehicle has to negotiate
  - road works
  - a construction site
  - lorry park

where an uneven surface may cause it to tilt over.

Material packed in plastic sacks and loaded on to pallets may be liable to slip — unless 'shrink-wrapped' or secured by banding.

However, material in canvass sacks may well remain totally stable (look at a potato merchant's load some time to see the difference).

Vehicles being carried 'piggy-back' must always have some form of chocks applied to their wheels in addition to a restraint — never rely on merely a handbrake holding them in place.

Remember that tubular loads — such as scaffolding poles, lamp standards, extrusions, girders, etc — may all move forward with some force if emergency braking occurs.

In such cases the headboard on the vehicle or semi-trailer can be demolished — with fatal results.

Dual purpose trailers have been developed which incorporate

- a 'belly tank', installed along the centre of the trailer, for transporting fluids
- a flatbed deck above for the conventional carriage of goods.

Obviously, in such instances, care must be taken not to rupture the tank below.

Types of restraint

Ropes

Traditionally, ropes have been the commonest method of securing both the load and sheets.

Ropes may be of fibre or modern 'man-made' materials such as nylon, polypropylene etc.

Whatever ropes are used, you should gain experience in the correct methods of securing the load.

The knots used are known in the trade as 'Dolly knots' which should only release when required (and not otherwise).

Additionally, ensure proper tension and only use the correct securing points.

Ropes are totally unsuitable for some loads — such as steel plates, scrap metal, etc.

Straps

These are generally made of webbing and are frequently used to secure many types of load.

Ensure that all straps, tensioners etc. are kept in good serviceable condition.

If the load has sharp edges straps can be used with suitable sleeves and corner protectors.

Battens and Chocks

Large, heavy objects such as metal ingots, castings, fabrications etc., should be chocked by nailing battens to the vehicle or trailer deck.

Chains

If there is any danger of either

– the weight of the load being too great for ropes or straps

or

– the load having sharp edges which would shear ropes or straps

then chains must be used, together with compatible tensioning devices.

Chains would provide added security when tree trunks or logs are being carried. Do not rely solely on vertical stanchions to hold the load.

Correct anchoring points

It is important that the correct anchoring points are employed, irrespective of the type of restraint being used.

The hooks fitted under some decks are only intended for fastening sheeting ropes.

Sheeting

Whenever sheets are used, whether tarpaulin, plastic, nylon or any other material — they must be secured in such a way that they do not start to flap and create a hazard for other road users.

When starting to cover a load, it is sensible to start with the rear-most sheet first — working forward.

This overlap will reduce the possibility of wind or rain being forced under the sheeting as the vehicle travels along in bad weather conditions.

All spare sheets and ropes must be tied down securely so that they do not fall into the path of following traffic.

Remember: Those coils of blue nylon rope lying on the roadway fell from somebody's vehicle!

You will need to use the same type of knots which remain taut in transit, but which can be released with the minimum of effort.

You will eventually appreciate this on a wet night in some windswept yard!

Whenever the driver climbs on to the vehicle or the load it is essential to follow the advice set out in Regulation 13

'loading or unloading vehicles'

in the document

'WORKPLACE HEALTH AND SAFETY'.

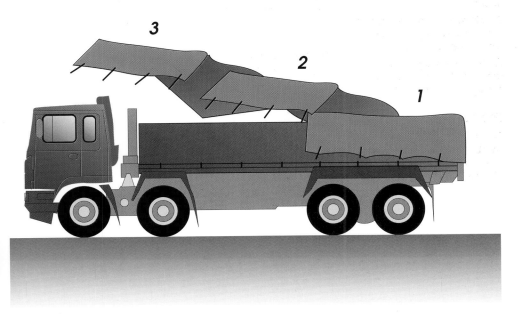

Curtainsides

The manufacturers of vehicles fitted with curtainside bodies are satisfied that a high degree of protection is given by the material used in their construction.

This does not relieve the driver of the responsibility for ensuring that the load is properly stowed and secured so that it will not move whilst in transit.

This is particularly important where there may be a 'multi-drop' load of varying materials — some of which may come under the hazardous materials classification.

Take notice of warnings of adverse weather conditions broadcast on the radio — especially if your vehicle is empty.

Under such conditions it is often safer to secure both curtain sides at one end of the vehicle — thus cutting down the wind resistance and removing the likelihood of being blown over or off the road.

Container lorries

ISO Cargo containers should only be carried on vehicles or trailers equipped with the appropriate securing points designed to lock into the container body.

Such vehicles may be intended for carrying

– a single 40ft (12m) container

– one or two 20ft (6m) containers

– larger numbers of smaller specially designed units (in modern use on de-mountable bodies).

Whatever type of container is carried, **all locking levers must be in the secured position during transit.**

Steel ISO containers should not be carried on flatbed platform vehicles where there are no means of locking the container in position.

Never rely on the weight of the container and its contents to hold it in place on a flat deck.

Ropes are totally inadequate to hold a typical sea-going steel container in place.

Skeletal vehicles or trailers have a main chassis-frame with outrigger supports into which the ISO container can be locked.

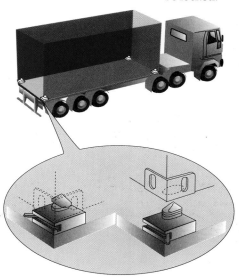

Environmental issues

The design of the vehicle can influence fuel consumption*

– cab mounted wind deflectors can effectively lower wind resistance created by large box bodies — together with lower side panel 'skirts'

– tipper bodies with prominent strengthening ribs on the outside can be plated-over to give improved performance.

– a fly sheet tightly fastened over the top of tipper bodies (especially when empty) can reduce the 'drag' effect.

* Further information can be found in the booklet published by the Department of Energy **'FUEL EFFICIENCY 20' Energy Efficiency in Road Transport.**

You, as the driver, have a part to play in helping to reduce the impact road transport has on the environment

– plan routes to avoid busy times and congestion

– anticipate well ahead

– avoid over-accelerating

– brake in good time

– reduce your overall speed

– avoid the need to 'make-up time'

– cover bulky loads with sheets to reduce wind resistance

– ensure maintenance schedules are strictly followed

  – filters changed

  – exhaust emissions meet current legal requirements

(members of the public are encouraged to report any vehicle emitting excessive exhaust fumes)

  – diesel engine injectors are operating efficiently

  – brakes correctly adjusted

  – tyre pressures correct.

Driving a 'green machine' does not just refer to the colour any more!

Road friendly suspension

Reference has already been made to the requirement that some form of road friendly suspension be fitted to vehicles which are intended to carry increased weights.

By replacing springs with some form of compressible material (usually air), a reduction in vibration caused by the impact of LGV wheels on road surfaces will reduce the damage to

– the road surface itself

– adjacent structures

– under-road services (gas,water,etc.)

– bridges

apart from the improvement to the quality of life for people living next to main roads carrying busy heavy traffic.

This system can in some instances be fitted retrospectively to vehicles, but it does mean that the vehicle will usually have to be equipped with additional compressed air storage tanks, creating some additional weight.

Damage to goods in transit

An increasing number of manufacturers are making use of the benefits which road friendly suspension gives in reducing damage to goods in transit.

Bulk Glass Carriers

Specialised semi-trailers used to carry consignments of sheet glass between the U.K. and Europe, and extensively on the continent, have no rear axles as such.

When loading takes place

– the hollow trailer body is backed to surround the racks (or stillage) holding the sheet glass load

– the body is then lowered into place

– the load is secured

– the body is raised into travelling position.

The whole process is carried out by controlling the sophisticated road friendly suspension system on each trailer wheel assembly.

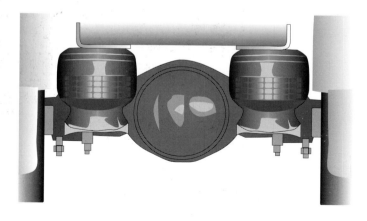

Diesel spillages

Because of the extremely slippery characteristics of diesel fuel, care must be taken at all times to avoid spillages.

Not only is it dangerous for anyone stepping on to it (especially getting down from a vehicle cab), but it creates a serious risk to other road users — especially motorcyclists.

Take care when refuelling. It is a legal requirement that all filler caps and tank hatches are properly closed and secure.

Alternative fuels

Diesel has traditionally been the fuel for LGV engines.

However, the possibility of using a number of alternative fuels is being explored.

Compressed Natural Gas (CNG)

While there are improvements in the quality of exhaust emissions produced, some of the technical disadvantages relate to the size and design of the vehicle fuel tanks required.

Methane

Because of the naturally occurring sources of this fuel, it is also being considered as a possible alternative to diesel oil which is a finite resource.

Hydrogen

This is another possible fuel source for road vehicles which is being studied

– again technical problems involve the storage of the highly inflammable gas.

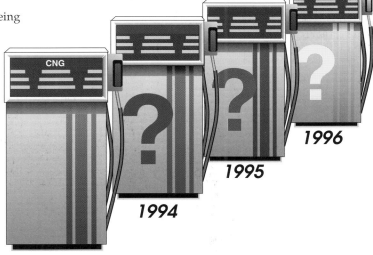

Audible warning systems

Remember that an audible warning system

– 'Vehicle Reversing' 'bleeper'

– horn

– verbal message etc.

must not be allowed to operate on a road subject to a 30 MPH speed limit between 23.30hrs and 07.00hrs.

Take care when setting any vehicle security alarm system.

As an LGV driver, it is up to you to recognise the effects your vehicle, and the way in which it is driven, can have on the environment around you!

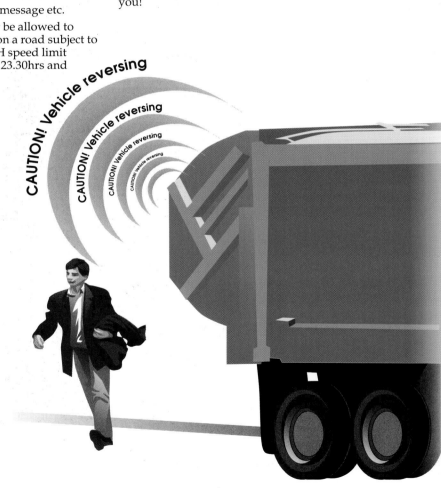

Legal Requirements

It is often said that, as a driver, you are one of the most closely regulated workers in industry today.

It is vital therefore, that you **constantly** keep up to date with the many changes in regulations which affect you.

European harmonisation programmes mean that long-standing regulations are either being modified or replaced.

It is for you to be sure that you comply with any regulations which affect

– your conduct
– your health
– your safety
– your licence
– your hours of work
– your vehicle
– your driving
– your load.

Never forget that ignorance is not accepted as a defence in law (even if the regulations changed yesterday!).

Conduct

Drugs

Drug abuse has now reached the point where well-known multinational companies have introduced random drug-testing for their drivers.

Drivers who fail such tests may face instant dismissal.

It should be obvious that you must not take any of the drugs which are generally accepted as 'banned substances' whilst driving

– Amphetamines (e.g. 'diet pills')

– Methylamphetamines MDMA

– Benzodiazapine (Tranquillizers)

– Methaqualone (Sleeping pills)

– Barbiturates (Sleeping pills)

– Propoxyphane

– Phencyclidine ('Angel Dust')

– Cannabis

– Cocaine

– Heroin

– Morphine/codeine.

Remember

Unlike alcohol (the effects of which last for about 24hrs) many of the effects of drugs can remain in the system for **up to 72 hrs**.

Simple 'Off the Shelf' Remedies

Even everyday cold or 'flu remedies can cause drowsiness.

Read the label carefully!

If in doubt, consult either your doctor or pharmacist.

If still in doubt
DO NOT DRIVE!

Alcohol

It is an offence to drive with more than

– a breath alcohol level in excess of 35 microgrammes per 100 ml

– a blood alcohol level in excess of 80 mg per 100 ml.

As the driver of a large goods vehicle you must not drink and drive.

If you are convicted of such an offence while driving an ordinary motor vehicle a driving ban will result in you losing your LGV entitlement and livelihood.

Be aware that alcohol may remain in the body's system for around 24 hours.

Not only can the effects on your reactions be evident the next morning — you could still fail a breath test!

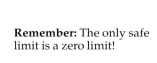

Remember: The only safe limit is a zero limit!

Health

Even apparently simple illnesses can affect your reactions.

You should be on your guard against the effects of

- 'flu symptoms
- hay fever
- a common cold
- tiredness and fatigue.

Falling asleep

Previously unexplained incidents where

- vehicles have left the road
- vehicles have collided with broken-down vehicles, Police patrol officers and other persons on the hard shoulder of motorways

have now been attributed to the phenomenon which has become known as the falling asleep at the wheel syndrome.

Be on your guard against boredom on comparatively empty roads or motorways, especially at night.

Always

- take planned rest stops
- keep a plentiful supply of fresh air circulating in the cab
- avoid allowing the cab to become unduly warm

- **avoid driving if you are not 100% fit to drive**
- avoid driving after a heavy meal.

Stop at the next layby or pull off the motorway (or slip road) if you start to feel tired.

The introduction of

- air suspension drivers' seats
- 'floating' cab suspension
- air suspension on vehicles
- quieter, smoother diesel engines
- more widely adopted sound-proofing materials

have all produced the improved 'cocoon' environment in which long-distance drivers spend the majority of their working hours.

This is a far cry from the cold, draughty, noisy, vibrating, rough-riding, 'through-flow' (holes) random ventilated vehicles that were in evidence on the roads only a comparatively short while ago.

However, there does seem to have been a price to pay for the 'progress' since those days.

DO NOT LET IT HAPPEN TO YOU.

Health and Safety Aspects

Many more activities have become the subject of Health & Safety regulations.

These include

– limits to the weight of objects which should be lifted manually e.g. loading packages

– provision of protective clothing, reflective jackets, boots, gloves, warm clothing and hard hats

where appropriate to the hazardous, or otherwise, nature of the work.

Asbestos

Drivers should be aware of the dangers to health from asbestos dust during maintenance, especially when dealing with dust from components known to contain this material

such as

– brake shoes

– clutch plates

– any tank or pipe lagging.

Safe Working Practice

Extra care must be taken when working

– near or over inspection pits (danger of falling)

– under hydraulically raised tipper bodies *(Use props!)*

– near engines emitting exhaust fumes (breathing problems)

– with solvents or degreasing agents (lung and skin problems)

– close to vehicle batteries (risk of burns or explosion)

– at the rear of a vehicle fitted with a 'tail-lift' mechanism (foot injuries)

– in, or near, paint spray shops (lung problems from vapour).

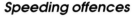

Driving licences

The LGV driving licence is a necessity if you wish to earn your living driving large goods vehicles.

It is essential that when you drive any vehicle other than a large goods vehicle your driving continues to be to the highest standards.

Remember, if you accumulate penalty points on your Category B licence, eventually your LGV licence will be at risk!

Speeding offences

Police forces and Local Authorities are now using the most up-to-date technology in efforts to persuade drivers to comply with speed limits.

At some locations fixed cameras have been installed which photograph vehicles exceeding the speed limit.

Improved detection equipment can now 'lock on' to individual vehicles in busy traffic flows.

New electronic systems now display the registration number and speed of any offending vehicle at selected motorway locations with a view to 'showing-up' the driver concerned.

Drivers whose speed is considerably higher than the legal speed limit can expect a proportionately higher penalty if a successful prosecution results.

The aim is to improve driving standards, not to increase prosecutions.

Red traffic light cameras

Cameras have been installed at many notorious accident blackspots to record drivers not complying with the traffic signals.

These are also intended to act as a deterrent and to improve safety for road users in general.

Remember: Whether it relates to an alleged speeding or traffic signal offence, any photograph produced as evidence which shows

– time

– date

– speed

– vehicle registration number

– time a red signal had already been showing

will prove difficult to dispute.

Drivers' hours

Currently, if you drive a goods vehicle over 3.5 Tonnes in the UK or European Union you must comply with EU drivers' hours rules.

The regulations governing drivers' hours fall into either

– British rules (if exempt from EU rules)

– European Union Rules.

For a list of exemptions from EU rules you are advised to study publications which give full particulars of all the legal requirements.

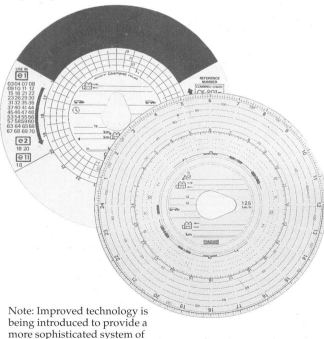

Note: Improved technology is being introduced to provide a more sophisticated system of monitoring.

Tachographs

EC Regulation 3821/85 requires a tachograph to be installed and used in vehicles registered in Member States and which are used for the carriage of passengers or goods by road.

The duty to ensure that the tachograph functions correctly rests with

– the employer

and

– **the driver.**

Drivers' Records

As the driver, you must comply with all the following requirements and complete and keep all appropriate records.

You must produce any records when requested to do so by an authorised officer

You must familiarise yourself with all relevant rules which govern

– definitions

– driving time

– breaks

– daily rest periods

– weekly rest periods

– exemptions

– the completion of records

– the production of records for examination — the retention of records

– the installation of tachographs

– the operation of tachographs

– offences relating to drivers' hours.

It is essential that you **thoroughly** understand the rules which relate to your permitted hours of work and the records which must be kept — since many of the prosecutions brought against LGV drivers relate to these subjects.

Your vehicle

You must ensure that the vehicle you drive complies with all regulations which relate to

– being legally roadworthy, including

– brakes

– lights

– tyres

– steering

– windscreen, wipers and washers

– horn

– mirrors

– speedometer

– tachograph

– number plates

– reflectors & reflective plates

– exhaust system

– any coupling gear

– speed limiter

– being correctly plated

– a current test certificate (if required)

– properly licensed with the appropriate valid disc(s) displayed

– insurance

– seatbelts*

– construction & use regulations

– any load being carried.

* Where seatbelts are fitted, THEY MUST BE WORN.

Remember that 'Red' diesel fuel is restricted to use for authorised purposes only.

Any driver whose vehicle is found to be illegally operating on this fuel will face severe penalties for attempting to evade excise duty.

Roadside checks are frequently carried out by HM Customs and Excise officers.

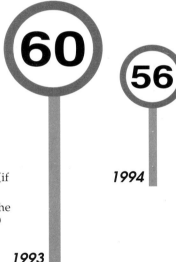

1994

1993

From 1994 speed limiters on certain vehicles will require setting or re-calibrating to 56 MPH

Speed Limiters as from 31 July 1993

• Articulated units over 16 tonnes (GVW), first registered on or after 1 January 1988

• Rigid goods vehicles over 16 tonnes (GVW) plated, constructed or adapted to tow a trailer exceeding 5 tonnes when laden first registered on or after 1 January 1988 capable of exceeding 60mph

must be fitted with a speed limiter set to a maximum of 60 mph.

New Vehicles

Goods vehicles over 7.5 tonnes (GVW) and capable of exceeding 60 mph have been required to be fitted with a speed limiter since 1 August 1992.

Exemptions

• Emergency vehicles used by

– Police forces

– Fire brigades

– Ambulance services

– mines rescue service

• Vehicles used by the armed forces

• Vehicles travelling less than 6 miles per week on public roads which are exempted from excise duty.

Your driving

You must at all times drive within the law and comply with

- speed limits
- weight limits
- loading/loading restrictions
- waiting restrictions
- stopping restrictions (clearways)
- lighting regulations
- restrictions of access to
  - pedestrian precincts
  - residential areas
  - traffic calming zones
  - play streets
- all traffic signs
- road markings
- traffic signals at
  - junctions
  - level crossings
  - fire or ambulance stations
  - lifting or swing bridges
- signals given by authorised persons
- Police officers
- traffic wardens
- Local Authority parking attendants (see 'Red Routes' in London, page 246)
- school crossing patrols
- persons engaged in road repairs
- motorway regulations
- regulations governing specific locations
  - tunnels
  - bridges
  - ferries
- pedestrian crossing rules.

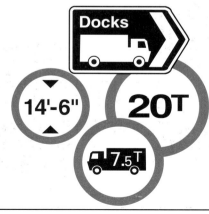

Your load

Any load, or part of it, must be carried in such a manner that it does not, at any time, endanger other road users and must be

- securely stowed
- within the weight limits permitted for your vehicle
- within the limits of size for the vehicle (unless clearly marked or proceeding under a special movement order under escort).

You must ensure that all devices for securing the load are effective

- all ropes, chains, straps are secure
- all sheets are fastened down
- all container locking handles are secured
- all doors, dropsides, tailgates are fastened

- any nets covering skips are in place
- all hatches on tank vehicles are closed to prevent spillage
- no material can fall from bulk cement vehicles
- any scrap metal is adequately secured and cannot fall off.

Anti-theft measures

Regrettably, instances of theft of vehicles, trailers, and loads take place every day.

It is your responsibility, as the driver in charge of the vehicle, to reduce the chances of it, or its contents, being stolen.

- Do not discuss details of your load with any unauthorised person
- Careless talk in the transport cafe may cost you your load or your vehicle.
- NEVER leave the keys in the cab while it is unattended — even if you are at the rear of the vehicle
- You cannot afford to give a lift to anyone — however plausible their story, or innocent they look
- So far as it is economical and convenient to do so, avoid using the same route and making the same drops wherever possible
- Have all major components (+glass) security etched with vehicle Reg. No.

- Only park in secure, well-lit, reputable overnight lorry parks if your rest stops can be planned this way
- One simple, but effective measure that many drivers adopt at overnight stops, is to park with the rear doors of your vehicle or its trailer/container hard up against another vehicle (this works well on most occasions)
- Keep your mobile telephone handset with you if one is available
- Avoid parking in obviously vulnerable areas if at all possible
- Ensure that all doors are locked and the windows secure if you sleep in the cab overnight
- Be aware that professional hijackers are extremely well-organised and may try to stop you by impersonating police officers — if in doubt, keep going to the nearest police station!

- Have an alarm system and/or immobiliser fitted to the vehicle by a reputable security specialist approved by the insurance company
- Avoid leaving any trailer unattended unless on approved secure premises
- Fit a kingpin lock to any trailer which has to be left unattended.

Operators are advised to

▶ Seek the advice of the local crime prevention officer — especially if engaged in the transit of high value merchandise
▶ Study the recommendations in British Standards 6803 which sets out

- Part 1 Specification for systems installed as original vehicle equipment
- Part 2 Code of Practice for systems installed after vehicle marketing
- Part 3 Code of Practice for the protection of goods in transit.

**No Truck...
No future!**
About 79% of stolen trucks are never found
Where are your trucks,
are they secure?

**Where's your
truck now?**
No truck...no job!

When to look
Truck thieves work most
nights, but Saturday night
is their clear favourite

Beware!
Three quarters of
truck thefts occur at
industrial estates

6. Vehicle characteristics

This section describes some of the main differences between the types of large goods vehicles on the roads today.

Every large goods vehicle has its own set of characteristics.

Even similar vehicles of the same model with the same type of engine etc. can handle and perform differently.

If you are going to drive larger vehicles safely you will need to appreciate the driving and handling techniques needed.

Contents

Vehicles shedding loads

'. . . and here is the latest Travel News with a warning for drivers using the A226 in Kent . . .
A lorry has shed its load . . .'

POLICE
ACCIDENT

Ask yourself **WHY?** Vehicles should not just shed loads
– only 'gritters' are designed to — and then not all at once!

6. Vehicle Characteristics

The causes are likely to have been

- Driving error
  - sudden change of speed or direction
  - too high a speed
  - skidding
- Instability of load
  - unsuitable vehicle
  - badly stowed
  - movement in load
  - restraints failed
  - unsuitable type of restraint
- Mechanical failure
  - suspension failure
  - tyre failure
  - trailer disengaged
  - wheel loss
- Collision
  - with another vehicle
  - with a bridge etc.
  - with street furniture
  - lamp posts
  - signs
  - signals
  - bollards.

Most of these situations are preventable.

Know the handling characteristics of your vehicle and drive in a safe and sensible manner.

Short wheelbase vehicles

- Will bounce more noticeably than some long wheelbase vehicles when empty. This can affect braking efficiency and all-round control.

- Are sometimes driven at excessively high speeds.

- Must not be pushed into bends or corners at higher speeds — simply because the vehicle *appears* to be easier to drive.

Long wheelbase Rigid Vehicles

Require additional room to manoeuvre, especially

- when turning left or right
- negotiating roundabouts
- entering or leaving premises.

Typical examples of this type of vehicle are

- removal vans
- box vans
- brick carriers
- bulk carriers (aggregates etc.)
- '8 wheeler' tankers.

In addition to the extra space needed when turning, the box type of body is very susceptible to cross winds on exposed stretches of road when lightly loaded or empty.

Failure to heed adverse weather conditions warnings may well result in the vehicle being blown over.

For this reason, high-sided vehicles are often banned from using certain roads and bridges where these problems are known to occur.

It is essential to observe any temporary speed limits imposed during these conditions.

Articulated Tanker vehicles

If

- The centre of gravity is high enough
- The vehicle is travelling sufficiently fast
- The vehicle is driven on a curved path

Initially, the vehicle wheels on the inside of the curve may start to lift. In many cases this is followed seconds later by roll-over.

Roll-over frequently involves tanker vehicles carrying fluids in bulk.

Under certain conditions, invariably on a curved path at moderate speeds (on roundabouts for instance) roll-over occurs.

The reasons for this problem have been attributed to a number of possible causes.

It appears most likely to occur when modern, heavier, more powerful vehicles, and, in the majority of cases, equipped with power steering, reach a critical situation.

As an example, the forces acting on a typical loaded articulated tanker vehicle negotiating a roundabout at a speed of about 25 MPH will cause it to overturn if only a further 1/4 turn is applied to the steering wheel.

You must be fully alert to the possibility of this happening.

Adjust the speed of your vehicle to avoid wheel lift followed in seconds by roll-over!

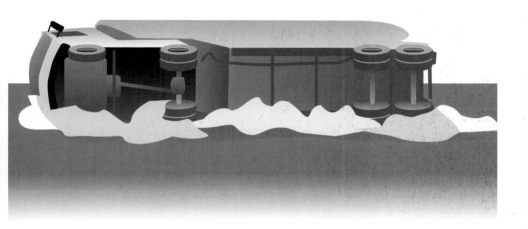

'Roll-over'

The type of suspension fitted to a vehicle will influence its resistance to roll.

Hence the installation of 'anti-roll' bars to some vehicles. Modern tri-axle semi-trailers fitted with single wheels on each side have extended the tracking width available compared to twin-wheeled units, and improved resistance to roll over.

Although vehicles equipped with air suspension systems are often considered to possess improved anti-roll stability compared to traditional steel leaf spring suspension, test results have shown that there are similarities in their level of stability.

What is important is that

*The transition from wheel-lift to roll-over is much more rapid on vehicles equipped with air suspension systems **giving very little warning that this is about to take place.***

Large petro-chemical companies provide specialised driver training to avoid such incidents happening.

Other safety factors

Tank vehicles without baffles fitted

If the drivers of certain tanker vehicles relax the footbrake when braking to a stop, there is a danger that the motion in the fluid load could force the vehicle forward.

This is due to the wave effect created in the tank contents, especially where baffle plates are omitted from the tank design (tanks for carrying foodstuffs or where cleaning out presents any difficulties).

Using walkways

Drivers of tanker vehicles must exercise special care when climbing on to walkways to gain access to tank hatches – not only to avoid injury as a result of slipping off, but also from the danger of overhead cables, pipeways etc.

Safety procedures

Venting

All tanks must be vented according to instructions in order to avoid serious damage to the tanker body itself due to the external air pressure becoming greater than the pressure within the tank.

Compressed gases

Drivers of vehicles carrying compressed gases — especially at low temperatures (liquid nitrogen, oxygen etc.) — must comply with regulations relating to the transport of such materials.

Risk of fire or explosion

In the case of hazardous materials, all safety precautions must be strictly followed — especially where there is a risk of fire or explosion.

The electrical systems of vehicles carrying petrochemicals and other highly inflammable materials are amended to meet stringent safety requirements.

No unauthorised additions or alterations must be made to such vehicles.

Any defects must be reported immediately.

The appropriate fire fighting equipment must be available, and drivers must be trained in its use.

Articulated Car Transporters

These vehicles require even higher standards of defensive driving and anticipation by the driver.

The overhang created by the top deck swinging through a greater arc than the cab of the tractive unit, particularly when negotiating a 90 degree turn, means the risk of collision with

– traffic signals

– lamp posts on centre refuges

– traffic signs

– walls and buildings

is even greater than with a normal LGV.

You must plan ahead and take an appropriate (avoiding) line on approach to turns when driving these vehicles.

It is too late when the top deck is already in contact!

The stability of these vehicles also needs to be considered — always remember it is a case of last on, first off — so that the lower deck may be clear of vehicles while there may be several still on top. The centre of gravity is substantially shifted in such cases.

The overall height **(especially when vans are being carried)** must be born in mind by the driver at all times.

Articulated Vehicles in general

Drivers of these vehicles must be especially vigilant before turning corners or negotiating roundabouts.

Failure to plan ahead and select the correct course will result in the rear wheels 'cutting-in', resulting in clipping the kerb at least, or colliding with street furniture, a pedestrian, cyclist, or another vehicle at worst.

You must avoid over-shooting left or right turns.

The stability of the vehicle is at risk if excessive steering lock is applied in order to make a 'swan-neck' turn.

Demountable bodies

Many of these are similar to containers, except that the body is fitted with 'legs' which can be lowered to enable the vehicle to drive under or out.

Care needs to be taken to ensure that

– the legs are secured in the down position before the vehicle is driven out

– the legs are secured in the up position before the vehicle moves off

– the height is correct and the body is stable before driving the carrier vehicle underneath

– a suitable firm level surface is available before 'demounting' the body.

Another type (often an open bulk high sided body) is fitted with skids and is winched up on to the carrying vehicle.

Apart from the dangers of overloading, care must be taken when operating such winches.

The construction of these vehicles often means that the centre of gravity can be higher than normal when conveying a loaded skip.

Take this into account — especially when cornering.

Double decked bodies

These vehicles are constructed to give increased carrying capacity to box van or curtainside bodies.

They are frequently used in the garment distribution sector.

Care must be taken to ensure that, as far as possible, the lower deck is not left empty while a load remains on the top tier with the vehicle in transit.

The resulting shift in the centre of gravity will result in the high-sided vehicle being even more vulnerable to the effect of crosswinds, and therefore more likely to overturn.

Refrigerated vehicles

When driving refrigerated or 'reefer' vehicles carrying suspended meat carcasses, care must be taken to avoid the 'pendulum' effect when cornering. Always reduce speed in good time.

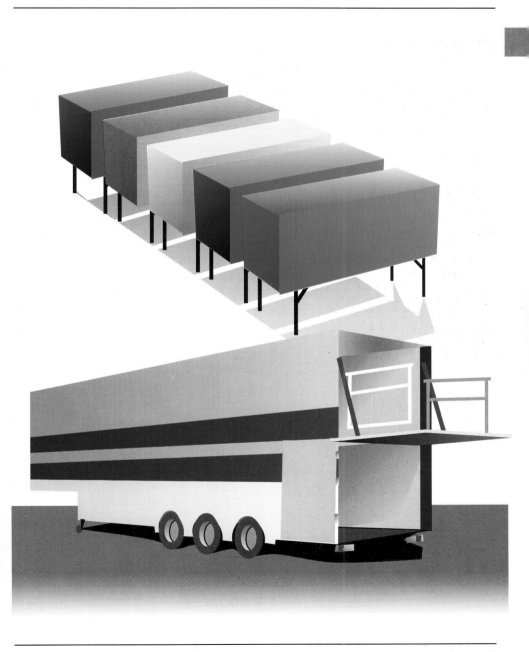

7. The recommended syllabus

As the driver of a large vehicle you must make safety your first priority

not just your own safety, but also that of other road users.

The information in this book describes and encourages safe driving techniques.

Whether you learn with an instructor (who may or may not have professional qualifications) or as 'work experience' with a colleague, you must be satisfied that you have fully covered all aspects of this syllabus.

Use this officially recommended syllabus as a check list to ensure your progress.

Contents

Driving in itself is a life skill, but driving a large goods vehicle is also the means by which you earn your living.

It may take many years to gain full mastery of the skills set out here, but you will need to aim for professional standards right from the very start.

This syllabus lists the skills which you must have in order to reach the high standards required to pass the driving test to become a professional lorry driver.

It is impossible to give details of all the rules and regulations which apply to both the driver and their vehicle in a book of this size.

However, you will need to know and keep up-to-date with current requirements.

If you learn with a training organisation, make sure they cover this syllabus fully.

If you learn through driving your employer's vehicle, it is essential that you cover the officially recommended syllabus.

Knowledge

You must have a **thorough** knowledge of

- The latest edition of The Highway Code, especially those sections which concern lorries

- Regulations governing drivers' permitted hours

- Regulations relating to the carriage of hazardous and other specialised goods.

You must also have a thorough understanding of

- General motoring regulations, especially
  - road traffic offences
  - licences, both drivers' and operators', where applicable (holding/ producing)
  - insurance requirements
  - vehicle road tax relating to LGVs (and any trailer) in your charge
  - plating of LGVs and their trailers
  - annual testing of LGVs.

1. Legal requirements

To learn to drive a large goods vehicle

You must

i   be at least 21 yrs old

ii   meet the stringent eyesight requirements

iii be medically fit to drive lorries

iv   hold a full motor car licence (Category B)

v   hold and comply with the conditions for holding either

   – a provisional LGV driving licence

   or

   – a full LGV driving licence for a lesser category of vehicle.

vi ensure that the vehicle
being driven is
  - legally roadworthy
  - correctly plated
  - has a current test
    (MOT) certificate
  - properly licensed with
    the correct tax disc
    displayed

vii make sure the vehicle
being driven is properly
insured for its use —
especially if it is on
contract hire

viii display L-plates to the
front and rear of the
vehicle

ix be accompanied by a
supervisor who holds a
valid full licence for the
category of vehicle
being driven

x   wear a seat belt, if fitted,
unless you are
exempted

Ensure that all seatbelts
in the vehicle, and their
anchorages and fittings,
are secure and free from
obvious defects.

Children should not
normally be carried in
LGVs. However, if a
child is carried in the
vehicle with permission,
you must comply with
all regulations relating
to the wearing of seat
belts by children or the
use of child restraints

xi be aware that it is a legal
requirement to notify
DVLC Swansea of any
medical condition
which could affect safe
driving if the duration is
likely to be three
months or more

xii ensure that any
adaptations are suitable
to control the vehicle
safely if the vehicle has
been adapted for any
disability.

2. Vehicle controls, equipment and components

You must

i   understand the function of the
    - accelerator
    - clutch
    - gears
    - footbrake
    - handbrake
    - secondary brake
    - steering
    and be able to use these competently

ii know the function of all other controls and switches on the vehicle and be able to use them competently

iii understand the meanings of
    - gauges
    - warning lights
    - warning buzzers
    - other displays on the instrument panel

iv be familiar with the operation of tachographs and their charts

v   know the legal requirements which apply to the vehicle
    - speed limits
    - weight limits
    - braking system (ABS)
    - fire extinguishers to be carried

vi be able to carry out routine safety checks, and identify defects, especially with
    - power steering
    - brakes (tractive unit + semi-trailer on articulated, or rigid vehicle + trailer, combinations)
    - tyres on all wheels
    - seatbelts
    - lights
    - reflectors/reflective plates
    - direction indicators
    - marker lights
    - windscreen, wipers and washers
    - horn
    - rear view mirrors
    - speedometer
    - tachograph
    - exhaust system
    - brake line and electric connections on rigid vehicles + trailers or articulated vehicles
    - coupling gear
    - hydraulic & lubricating systems
    - self-loading or tailgate equipment
    - dropside hinges and tailgate fastenings
    - curtainside fittings/fastenings
    - winches or auxiliary gear
    where these items are fitted

vii know the safety factors relating to
    - stowage
    - loading
    - stability
    - restraint of any load carried on the vehicle

viii know the effects speed limiters will have on the control of your vehicle – especially when you intend to overtake

ix know the principles of the various systems of retarders which may be fitted to LGVs
    - electric
    - engine driven
    - exhaust brakes
    and when they should be brought into operation.

3. Road user behaviour

You must

i   know the most common causes of road traffic accidents

ii   know which road users are more vulnerable and how to reduce the risks to them

iii know the rules, risks and effects of drinking and driving

iv   know the effects that
     – illnesses (even minor ones)
     – drugs or cold remedies
     – fatigue,
     can have on a driver's performance

v   recognise the importance of complying with rest period regulations

vi   be aware of the age-dependent problems among other road users
     – children
     – young cyclists
     – young drivers
     – more elderly drivers
     – elderly or infirm pedestrians

vii concentrate and plan ahead in order to anticipate the likely actions of other road users and be able to select the safest course of action.

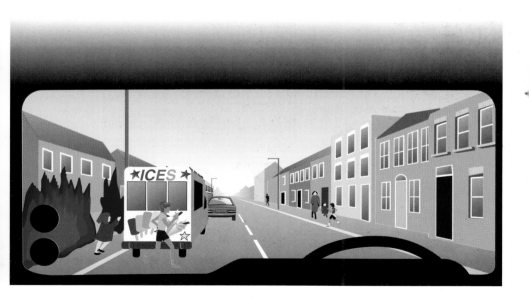

4. Vehicle characteristics

You must

i know the most important principles concerning braking distances under various

– road

– weather

– loading

conditions

ii know the different handling characteristics of other vehicles with regard to

– speed

– stability

– braking

– manoeuvrability

iii know that some other vehicles such as bicycles and motorcycles are less easily seen than others

iv be aware of the difficulties caused by the characteristics of both your own, and other vehicles, and be able to take the appropriate action to reduce any risks which may arise.

Examples are

– large goods vehicles and buses moving to the right before making a sharp left turn

– drivers of articulated vehicles having to take what appears to be an incorrect line before negotiating

   – corners

   – roundabouts

   – entrances

– blind spots which occur on many large vehicles

– bicycles, motorcycles and high-sided vehicles being buffeted in strong winds, especially on exposed sections of road

– turbulence created by large goods vehicles travelling at speed affecting pedestrians, cyclists, motorcyclists, vehicles towing caravans, and drivers of smaller motor vehicles.

At all times remember that other road users may not understand the techniques required in order to manoeuvre a large goods vehicle safely.

5. Road and weather conditions

You must

i   know the various hazards which can arise when driving

- in strong sunlight
- at dusk or dawn
- during the hours of darkness
- on various types of road such as
  - narrow lanes in rural areas
  - one-way streets
  - two-way roads in built-up areas
  - three lane roads
  - dual carriageways with various speed limits
  - trunk roads with two-way traffic
  - motorways

ii   gain experience in driving on urban roads with 20 or 30 MPH speed limits, and also on roads carrying denser traffic volumes at higher speed limits in both daylight and during the hours of darkness

iii   gain experience in driving on both urban and rural motorways

iv   know which road surfaces will provide better or poorer grip when braking

v   know all the associated hazards caused by bad weather such as

- rain
- snow
- ice
- fog

vi   be able to assess the difficulties caused by

- road
- traffic
- weather conditions

vii   drive defensively and anticipate how the prevailing conditions may affect the standard of driving shown by other road users.

6. Traffic signs, rules and regulations

You must

i   have a thorough knowledge and understanding of the meanings of traffic signs and road markings

ii   you must be able to recognise and comply with traffic signs such as

- weight limits
- height limits
- signs prohibiting LGVs
- loading/unloading restrictions
- traffic calming measures
  - 20 MPH zones
  - road width restrictions
  - speed reduction humps
- roads designated 'Red Routes'
- night-time and week-end lorry bans such as those in the London Boroughs.

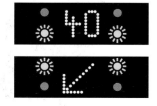

7. Vehicle control and road procedure

You must have the knowledge and skill to carry out the following list of tasks when appropriate

– safely and expertly

– in daylight and, if necessary, during the hours of darkness.

Where the tasks involve other road users you must

– make proper use of the mirrors

– take effective observation

– give signals where necessary.

i   take the following necessary precautions, where they are applicable, before getting into the vehicle

– ensure number plates are correct and securely fitted

– check all round for obstructions

– ensure that any load is secure

– check air lines are correctly fitted and free from leaks

– check all couplings to drawing vehicle and trailer

– check landing gear is raised

– check trailer brake is released

– check all bulbs, lenses and reflectors are fitted

– make sure all lights, indicators and stop lights are working

– ensure all reflective plates are visible, clean and secure

– examine tyres for defects

– examine all load restraints for tension etc.

– ensure any unused ropes are safely stowed.

ii   before leaving the vehicle cab make sure that

– the vehicle is stopped in a safe, legal and secure place

– the handbrake is on

– the engine is stopped

– the electrical system is switched off

– the gear lever / selector is in neutral

– all windows are closed

– the passenger door is secure

– the keys have been removed from the starter switch

– you will not endanger anyone when you open the door.

iii before starting the engine, carry out the following safety checks

- the handbrake is applied
- the gear lever is in neutral
- the doors are properly closed
- your seat is adjusted for
  - height
  - distance from the controls
  - back rest support and comfort
- the mirrors are correctly adjusted
- your seatbelt is fastened and adjusted.

iv start the engine, but before moving off check

- the vehicle (and any trailer) lights are on, if required
- gauges indicate correct pressures for braking system
- no warning lights are showing
- no warning buzzer is operating

- no ABS fault indicator is lit (where fitted)
- all fuel and temperature gauges are operating normally
- engine pre-heater (glow plug) lamp is operating (where fitted)
- it is safe to move off by looking all round — especially the blind spots.

Part 1 Before the LGV Driving Test

Vehicle Control and road procedure

(contd.)

v   move off
     – straight ahead
     – at an angle
     – on the level
     – uphill
     – downhill.

vi   select the correct road position for normal driving.

vii take effective observation in all traffic conditions.

viii drive at a speed appropriate to the road, traffic and weather conditions.

ix   anticipate changes in traffic conditions, adopt the correct action at all times and exercise vehicle sympathy.

x   move into the appropriate traffic lane correctly and in good time.

xi   pass stationary vehicles safely.

xii meet, overtake and cross the path of other vehicles safely.

xiii turn right or left at
     – junctions
     – crossroads
     – roundabouts.

xiv drive ahead at
     – crossroads
     – roundabouts.

xv   keep a safe separation gap when following other vehicles.

xvi act correctly at all types of pedestrian crossing.

xvii show proper regard for the safety of all other road users, with particular respect for those most vulnerable

xviii drive on
     – urban roads
     – rural roads
     – dual carriageways
     keeping up with the traffic flow (but still observing speed limits) where it is safe and appropriate to do so.

xix comply with
     – traffic regulations
     – traffic signs
     – signals given by authorised persons
     – Police officers
     – traffic wardens
     – school crossing patrols.

xx   take the correct action on signals given by other road users.

xxi stop the vehicle safely at all times.

xxii select safe and suitable places to stop the vehicle reasonably close to the nearside kerb when requested
  – on the level
  – facing uphill
  – facing downhill
  – before reaching a parked vehicle, but leaving sufficient room to move away again.

xxiii stop the vehicle on the braking exercise manoeuvring area
  – safely
  – as quickly as possible
  – under full control
  – within a reasonable distance from a designated point.

xxiv reverse the vehicle on the manoeuvring area
  – under control
  – with effective observation
  – on a pre-determined course
  – to enter a restricted opening
  – to stop with the extreme rear of the vehicle within a clearly defined area.

xxv cross all types of level crossings
  – railway
  – rapid transit systems (trams) where appropriate.

8. Additional knowledge

You must know

i the importance of inspecting all tyres on the vehicle for

 – correct pressure

 – signs of wear

 – evidence of damage

 – safe tread depth

 – objects between twin tyres

 – indications of overheating.

ii safe driving principles in order to prevent skids occurring.

iii how to drive when the road is

 – icy

 – snow-covered

 – flooded

 – covered by excess surface water.

iv what to do if you are involved in

 – a damage-only traffic accident

 – a road traffic accident involving

  – injury

  – fire

  – spillage of hazardous material

  – danger to other road users due obstruction by fallen loads etc.

 – any type of accident on a motorway

v steps to take if your vehicle breaks down

 – in the day time

 – at night

on

 – a bend on a road with two-way traffic

 – a busy dual carriageway

 – a clearway

 – a motorway.

vi the differences between toughened and laminated glass used in LGV windscreens.

vii how to use the hammer or similar tool, if fitted, to exit from the vehicle in an emergency.

viii basic First Aid for use on the road.

ix the precautions to take to prevent theft of

 – the vehicle

 – the load

 – a trailer

 – equipment on the vehicle.

x factors to consider when selecting a safe place to leave an unattended trailer or semi-trailer

 – legal (i.e. not a public road)

 – safe (will not endanger any member of the public)

 – convenient (not blocking any access or exit)

 – suitable (level and firm enough to support the trailer or semi-trailer)

 – secure (the trailer and/or its load will not be liable to be stolen)

 – will not create a hazard for other road users

 – whether any anti-theft device can be fitted (e.g. coupling locking device).

9. Motorway driving

You must have a thorough **practical** knowledge of the special

– rules

– regulations

– driving techniques

which apply to motorways.

You will not be asked to drive on the motorway on your LGV driving test, but will be expected to show a thorough understanding and and knowledge of all aspects of motorway driving.

In particular

– overtaking

– exercising lane discipline

– the effects of speed limiters

– joining and leaving motorways

– breakdown and emergency procedures

– driving in adverse weather conditions

– principal causes of accidents on motorways.

10. Safe working Practices

i   adopt the correct method of climbing into the vehicle cab.

ii   avoid the risks involved by jumping down from the cab.

iii ensure any tilt cab locking mechanism is secure (especially after routine maintenance).

iv   follow safety guide-lines when operating

– under raised tipper bodies

– near inspection pits

– tail-lift controls

– on-board hoists

– on any walkway

– under overhead cables

– refuelling points

– between parked vehicles

– between tractive unit and trailer of any kind

– underneath any vehicle

– under any vehicle supported by jacks

or before

– carrying out roadside repairs

– removing road wheels

– inflating tyres.

8. Applying for the LGV Driving Test

The standard required to pass the LGV driving test is a high one.

However, if you are properly prepared, cover the officially recommended syllabus and combine this with practice on a wide variety of roads in different traffic conditions, your driving should be well above the standard required.

Several aspects relating to training are covered in this section, in addition to giving details of application forms, block-booking arrangements etc.

The section also provides background information about the test, as well as describing the content of the test itself in detail.

Contents

Getting training

Choosing a training organisation

There is no DSA register of approved instructors who teach pupils how to drive a large goods vehicle, unlike learning to drive a motor car.

However, there are a number of training organisations recognised by the principal bodies concerned with road haulage, who have established the highest standards of training for the vocational licence.

The leading organisation for training drivers to drive large goods vehicles was formerly RTITB which is now known as Road Transport Industry Training and Business Services Ltd.

You can find details of a local training group by contacting the road haulage industry organisations (Freight Transport Association Ltd., Road Haulage Association,) whose addresses are given at the end of this book.

Covering the syllabus

Whether you select one of these training groups, or an individual trainer with perhaps only one vehicle, it is essential that all aspects of the syllabus set out in Section 7 are covered.

Comprehensive training

It is in your own interests to find out how comprehensive the course will be before you enrol.

Obviously the opportunity to drive a variety of vehicles will widen your knowledge and understanding of large goods vehicles.

If you intend to drive articulated vehicles, it is essential that you have the opportunity to gain *practical* experience of uncoupling and re-coupling units in this category.

Loaded vehicles and 'Roping & Sheeting'

Valuable experience can be gained from driving loaded vehicles under supervision.

By doing so you will appreciate the marked difference in handling characteristics between driving an unladen vehicle and one which is fully loaded.

Additionally, you should seek opportunities to learn the correct methods of load restraint (including 'roping & sheeting').

You will need to make enquiries, either from successful pupils, or from the trainers offering LGV tuition.

If the training organisation is able to give you details of companies using their services, this will help you to choose an instructor or organisation with an established reputation for quality of instruction and proven LGV test results.

8. Applying for the Large Goods Vehicle Driving Test

Training

Your training should cover driving

- On as many different types of road as possible

- In all sorts of traffic conditions, including darkness

- On dual carriageways where the upper speed limit (50 MPH) for LGVs applies.

You will probably be asked to drive on such roads during the LGV test.

Motorways

Although LGV learner drivers are permitted to drive on motorways you will not be expected to do so on the LGV driving test.

It is in your interests to gain experience of motorway driving while still under supervision.

You will be expected to answer questions which demonstrate that you have a **thorough** understanding of motorway rules — in particular, those which affect LGV drivers.

Practice

You should have the opportunity to practise the braking and the reversing exercises on a suitable off-road site.

Avoid concentrating solely on them.

What to avoid when you practise

- Creating undue inconvenience for others.

  Not all road users appreciate the difficulties which an LGV driver faces when manoeuvring a large vehicle, especially

  - moving off

  - stopping

  - turning left or right

  - in narrow roads

- Causing nuisance to residents and other traffic.

If a local problem already exists due to LGV training taking place, avoid making the situation worse.

Your trainer should be aware of any such difficulties and should use an alternative area to practise.

The continuous noise created by

- the hissing of air brakes

- revving the engine to build-up air pressure

- persistent stopping and starting

can soon become a reason for complaint in residential areas.

Where to train

If possible, choose areas such as industrial estates or business parks — preferably outside normal working hours.

(This will often depend on your trainer and the periods when the vehicle is available).

Choose your training areas with care so that you cause minimum interference to the local traffic, businesses, and residents.

By doing so, you will reduce resistance to LGV training taking place in that area.

About the LGV driving test

You should aim for a professional standard.

You will pass if the examiner sees that you can

- Drive safely to a high standard

- Show expert handling of all controls

- Carry out the set exercises accurately and under control

- Show a thorough knowledge of The Highway Code and vehicle safety matters.

Test routes

- Are as uniform as possible

- Include a wide range of typical road and traffic conditions.

Uniform standards

Examiners are trained to carry out tests to the same high standards nationally.

You should have the same results from different examiners or at different LGV Driving Test Centres.

A DSA supervising officer may sit in on your test if there are more than two seats in the cab of your vehicle.

Do not let this worry you.

The supervising officer will not be examining you, but making sure the examiner is carrying out the test properly.

Since the supervising officer will not interfere with the test or the result, just carry on as if he (or she) was not there.

Presence of trainers during the test

Because so many LGV cabs have only two seats, it is not usually possible for any one else to be present.

If there are three or more seats in the cab of your vehicle, and provided a DSA supervising officer is not intending to observe the test, your instructor is allowed to be present during the test — if you wish, but must not take any part in it.

8. Applying for the Large Goods Vehicle Driving Test

What the examiner will be looking for

The examiner will want to see you drive safely to a high standard under various road and traffic conditions.

He (or she) will

- Ask you to carry out set exercises
- Give you directions clearly and in good time.

The examiner will be understanding and sympathetic, and will make every effort to put you at your ease.

Examiners appreciate that there may be a higher noise level in some vehicles, and will make sure that you can hear any instructions or directions clearly.

To avoid distracting you, the examiner will not engage you in any unnecessary conversation while you are busy driving.

Your performance

Drive in the way your instructor has taught you.

If you make a mistake, try not to worry. It might be minor and may not affect the result of the test.

The examiner will be looking for an overall high standard and you are unlikely to fail for one or two minor mistakes.

Duration of the test

The test will take a total time of around 1½ hours.

What the test consists of

Apart from general driving, which will be described in more detail in Section 9, the test will include

- Special exercises, such as
  - reversing within a marked area into a restricted opening
  - a braking exercise
  - a gear changing exercise
  - moving off on the level, at an angle, uphill, and downhill.
- Questions on
  - The Highway Code
  - other matters relating to safe operation and driving

are usually asked at the end of the test.

Category C + E vehicles

Specific questions relating to the uncoupling and re-coupling of either

- drawbar trailers or
- semi-trailers

are usually asked at the start of the test.

Special Exercises

Two of the special exercises are always carried out on site at the LGV driving test centre.

These are

- the reversing exercise
- the braking exercise.

The remainder of the special exercises will take place during the road section of the test.

Make sure you understand what is being asked of you

The examiner will be as helpful as possible, and will explain what is required by showing you a diagram of the exercises and then ask you to carry them out.

If you are unsure about anything, ask! The examiner will explain again.

During the reversing exercise, the examiner will remain outside the vehicle.

However, the examiner will join you in the cab before explaining the braking exercise to you and will watch your handling of the controls when you carry out the exercise.

Make sure you understand what is required!

The braking exercise is *always* carried out before leaving the LGV driving test centre. If your vehicle does not pull up satisfactorily, the examiner may decide not to continue the test in the interests of safety.

8. Applying for the Large Goods Vehicle Driving Test

The Highway Code

You must

- Know and understand The Highway Code **thoroughly**

- Obey it during the test

- Answer questions on it.

So study the latest edition carefully!

Special circumstances

To make sure that enough time is allowed for your test, it would help the DSA to know

- If you are restricted in any way in your movements

- If you have any disability which may affect your driving

So, please include this information on your test application form.

Drivers with Disabilities

Whatever the nature of your disability you will still take the same LGV driving test as every other candidate.

Your examiner may wish to talk to you about your disability and any adaptations fitted to your vehicle.

For this reason, it is important to give details of your disability when you apply for your test.

If you would like further information, please see the list of useful addresses at the back of this book.

Language difficulties

If you have difficulty speaking or understanding English, you are allowed to bring an interpreter who must not be your instructor (provided your vehicle has more than two seats in the cab).

Saturday tests

Saturday tests are available at some LGV Driving Test Centres.

The fees are higher than for a test during normal working hours on weekdays.

You can get details from

- DSA Regional Offices

- LGV Driving Test Centres.

8. Applying for the Large Goods Vehicle Driving Test

Applying for the LGV Driving Test

You must already have entitlement to drive LGVs (either a LGV Provisional licence, or a full licence for a lower group than the category you wish to be tested on) before applying for the test.

Apply in good time, but only when you are sure your driving has reached the standards set out in this book.

You should ensure that you receive first class instruction — together with as much practice as possible.

Only when you are driving

• Consistently well

• With confidence

• In complete control

• Without assistance and guidance from your instructor

will you be really ready for your LGV driving test.

Most people fail the test because they have not had enough instruction and practice.

Ensure that all aspects of the recommended syllabus for learning to drive LGVs have been fully covered (see Section 7).

Application Form

You can obtain an application form (DLV 26) for the driving test from any DSA Regional Office (see list of addresses at the back of this book).

Study the guidance notes carefully, including the table of large goods vehicle categories, especially if you wish to drive more than one category of large goods vehicle.

Make sure you give all the particulars asked for on the application form (especially your driving licence details) otherwise the form will only have to be returned to you, and your driving test appointment will be delayed.

Send the correct fee with your application.

• Cheques

or

• Postal Orders

should be crossed & made payable to 'Driving Standards Agency'.

If you send a Postal Order, keep the counterfoil.

Do not send cash

Send your application to DSA at least 28 days before your preferred date for test (in summer, longer notice is often helpful due to increased demand).

Programmes of tests are arranged well in advance and, if you do not give enough notice, you may not be given your preferred date.

Send your application to the appropriate DSA Regional Office.

Remember:

• Address your application correctly

• Only post it to the DSA Regional Office

• Enclose the correct fee

otherwise your application will be delayed.

Part 2 The Large Goods Vehicle Driving Test

Form DLV26

DRIVING STANDARDS AGENCY

Application for a Large Goods Vehicle (LGV) or Passenger Carrying Vehicle (PCV) Driving Test Appointment

For Official Use Only

DD	MM	YY	FTA	DD	MM	YY	FTA	DD	MM	YY	FTA	Accounts Use Only

Time | Time | Time
Card | Card | Card

Please read the notes overleaf before completing this form.

Ordinary Driving Licence Details

Driver No

Type of Licence
(please tick one box)   Provisional ☐   Full ☐

Vocational Licence Held (please tick)

LGV ☐   Provisional ☐   Full ☐

PCV ☐   Provisional ☐   Full ☐

Expiry Date

Categories held

Personal Details

Surname

First name and Initial(s)

Address

Postcode

☎ Home   Work

Disabilities and Special Circumstances

Details of Test Appointment

Choice of Centre

Unacceptable Days (tick any days you are unavailable)	Mon		Tue		Wed		Thur		Fri		Sat	
	am	pm	am	pm	am	pm	am	pm	am	pm	am	pm

Unacceptable Dates (enter details)

Earliest Date you will be available for test	Day	Month	Year

DLV 26

Test Vehicle Details

(please tick category)

Large Goods Vehicles

		Man	Auto
Goods vehicles over 7.5 tonnes	C		
Articulated goods vehicles over 7.5 tonnes	C+E		
Goods vehicle and trailer combination of at least 15 tonnes gross	C+E		

Cab Seating Capacity

Overall Dimensions (metres)

Length   Height   Width

Passenger Vehicles

		Man	Auto
All vehicles 8 passenger seats or more, **less** than 8.5 metres in length	D (limited to 16 passenger seats)		
All vehicles 8 passenger seats or more, 8.5 metres or **more** in length.	D		
All vehicles 8 passenger seats or more, 8.5 metres or more in length (with trailer over 1250 kg gross).	D+E		

Important: See notes overleaf

Fee enclosed   £

Cheque/postal order No

Signed

Date

Please fill in this box so that your appointment card can be sent to you.

Name

Address

Postcode

Block Booking arrangements

(Formerly Forms 'X,Y,Z')

Some LGV driver training organisations are able to make advance bookings for LGV driving tests.

The application form consists of two sheets, DLV26A & B, which must be submitted to the DSA Regional Office at least one calendar month before the preferred test date.

This simply reserves an appointment, and no candidate's details are included at this stage.

The DSA Regional Office LGV booking section will return Form DLV26A (Part 2 only) attached to DLV26B to the LGV training organisation confirming the appointment.

Parts 3 & 4 of Form DLV26B must be completed and delivered to the centre where the test is to take place *no later than 4 pm on the working day prior to the test appointment.*

The training organisation must ensure that the candidate's personal details, licensing details (ordinary and LGV), *and signature* are included on Part 4 of Form DLV26B.

If these details are omitted the examiner may not be able to conduct the test.

Form DLV26A (Parts 1 & 2)

DRIVING
STANDARDS
AGENCY

Application for a Large Goods Vehicle (LGV) or Passenger Carrying Vehicle (PCV) Driving Test Appointment under a Block Booking Arrangement

For Official Use Only			
DD MM YY FTA	DD MM YY FTA	DD MM YY FTA	Accounts Use Only
Time	Time	Time	
Card	Card	Card	

In accordance with the Block Booking Guidlines this form, completed only at part 1, must reach the DSA Regional Office with the fee, **at least one calendar month** before the date of appointment. Otherwise, any provisional booking by the training organisation will be made available to another candidate.

Part 1   Details of Reservation

Reserving Organisation Details

Name

Address

Post Code

☎

Appointment Details

Date   Time   am/pm

Test Centre

Fee enclosed £   Cheque/Postal Order No

Signature

Signature   Date

- -

Part 2   Confirmation - To be filled in by the DSA Regional Office

This appointment has been confirmed.

Date   Time   am/pm

Test Centre

Please keep this slip as confirmation of your appointment details.

DLV 26A (Rev 3/93)

8. Applying for the Large Goods Vehicle Driving Test

Form DLV26B (Parts 1 & 2)

DRIVING STANDARDS AGENCY

Application for a Large Goods Vehicle (LGV) or Passenger Carrying Vehicle (PCV) Driving Test Appointment under a Block Booking Arrangement

For Official Use Only												
DD	MM	YY	FTA	DD	MM	YY	FTA	DD	MM	YY	FTA	Accounts Use Only
Time			Time				Time					
Card			Card				Card					

Part 1 Details of Reservation

Reserving Organisation Details

Name

Address

Post Code

☎

Appointment Details

Date   Time   am/pm

Test Centre

Fee enclosed £   Cheque/Postal Order No

Signature

Signature   Date

Part 2 Confirmation - To be filled in by the DSA Regional Office

This appointment has been confirmed.

Date   Time   am/pm

Test Centre

Please complete the details overleaf and deliver this form to the centre where the test is to take place **no later than 4 pm on the working day prior to the test appointment.**

Any failure to notify examiners of candidates and vehicle details will be considered to be a breach of the DSA block booking agreement with your organisation.

The DSA reserves the right to withdraw the provisional reservations facility if the terms of the agreement are breached.

DLV 26B (Rev 3/93)

Form DLV26B (Parts 3 & 4)

Part 3 Test Vehicle Details

Test Vehicle Details

(please tick category)

			Man	Auto
Large Goods Vehicles	Goods vehicles over 7.5 tonnes	C		
	Articulated goods vehicles over 7.5 tonnes	C+E		
	Goods vehicle and trailer combination of at least 15 tonnes gross	C+E		

Cab Seating Capacity for LGVs [   ]

Overall Dimensions Length [   ] Height [   ] Width [   ]

			Man	Auto
Passenger Vehicles	All vehicles 9 passenger seats or more, **less** than 8.5 metres in length	D (limited to 16 passenger seats)		
	All vehicles 9 passenger seats or more, 8.5 metres or **more** in length	D		
	All vehicles 9 passenger seats or more, 8.5 metres or more in length (with trailer over 1250 kg gross)	D+E		

Part 4 Trainee / Licensing Details

The candidate must hold a valid vocational driving licence at the time of the test.

Personal Details

Surname [   ]

First name and Initial(s) [   ]

Address [   ]

Postcode [   ]

☎ Home [   ] Work [   ]

Licensing Details

Ordinary Driving Licence No [| | | | | | | | | | | | | | | |]

Type of Licence Provisional [ ] Full [ ]

Vocational Licence Entitlement

LGV (HGV) [ ] Provisional [ ] Categories held [   ]
Full [ ] Expiry Date [   ]

PCV (PSV) [ ] Provisional [ ] Categories held [   ]
Full [ ] Expiry Date [   ]

Trainee's Signature

Signature [   ] Date [   ]

The Test Appointment

When your application has been received you will be sent notification.

This also acts as a receipt for your fee.

It will give the date, time and place of your appointment.

Check your appointment notification as soon as you receive it to make sure the date and time of the test appointment are suitable.

If you do not receive notification after 21 days, contact the DSA Regional Office as soon as possible.

Note: If your appointment was made under block-booking arrangements, you will not receive notification direct.

Cancellations

If you cannot keep the appointment, you should notify the DSA Regional Office immediately and return your appointment notification.

You must give at least **5** clear (working) days' notice, otherwise you will forfeit your fee and will have to re-apply with another fee.

Note: 5 clear days means an interval of 5 whole working days

– not counting the day DSA Regional Office receives your notification

– not counting the day of your test

Change of Address

Please notify the DSA Regional Office immediately if you change your address before the day of your appointment.

Change of Vehicle

Please notify the DSA Regional Office if you have to bring a different vehicle from the one described on your application form in order to avoid delay when you arrive for your test.

Inform the senior driving examiner at the test centre, either beforehand, or as soon as you arrive, if there is any last-minute change of vehicle.

9. The LGV driving test

To drive a large goods vehicle unaccompanied, you must first pass the LGV driving test.

It is not just a longer version of the car driving test which the learner driver faces — you will be expected to drive in a thoroughly expert and professional manner.

This section sets out the main requirements of the test.

Contents

Content of the test

The test lasts approximately one and a half hours and consists of:

- Special exercises carried out on the test area at the driving test centre
  - a reversing exercise
  - a braking exercise.

- A drive, including a wide variety of road and traffic conditions, of approximately one hour's duration

  The route will take in roads carrying two-way traffic, dual carriageways and, where possible, one-way systems.

  A gear-changing exercise will usually be carried out at the earliest convenient location during the on-the-road phase.

  You will be expected to demonstrate that you can move off smoothly and safely both uphill and downhill, in addition to moving off normally ahead and at an angle.

You will need to show that you can safely

- meet other vehicles
- overtake
- cross the path of other vehicles
- keep a safe separation distance
- negotiate various types of roundabouts
- exercise correct lane discipline
- display courtesy and consideration to other road users especially
  - pedestrians
  - riders on horseback
  - cyclists
  - motorcyclists
- apply the correct procedure at

  pedestrian crossings
  - level crossings (both railway and tramway — where appropriate)
  - traffic signals
  - road junctions.

You will need to show

- **effective** use of the mirrors
- correct use of signals
- alertness and anticipation
- correct use of speed
- observance of speed limits
- vehicle sympathy.

- Questions on
  — The Highway Code
  — other matters relating to safe operation and driving.

Note: Candidates who are driving either an articulated LGV, or a rigid vehicle plus trailer combination, will be asked questions relating to coupling and uncoupling procedures before the reversing exercise.

Attending for the test

LGV driving tests are conducted to a strict timetable.

Make sure you arrive in good time — otherwise your test cannot be taken and you will lose your fee.

Remember: The test will last for 1½ hrs — make sure that you will not exceed the number of hours you are allowed to drive by law.

Note: From 1 April 1994 you will be asked to sign a declaration that the vehicle is properly insured for the purposes for which it is being used.

This declaration will be incorporated on the Driving Test Report Form DLV 25.

Your Licences

Make sure you have

– your full motor car licence

– the appropriate LGV licence entitlement

Provisional

or

Full LGV (or HGV) for a lower category

with you.

You will be asked to show them to the examiner.

Remember

It is your responsibility to ensure that you have the appropriate licence entitlement.

If you have any reason to believe you may not be granted a licence to drive LGVs

or

Your licence has been returned to DVLC Swansea for any reason, you must inform the examiner **before** the start of the test.

If you attend for the driving test without your driving licence/s with you, the examiner will ask you for some other form of identity

Any of the following are acceptable:

• A signed driving licence issued in any other country

– provided it bears the holder's name in the roman alphabet and your photograph

• A signed passport

• A signed International Driving Permit

• A signed British Forces driving licence

• A signed identity card issued by your employer

This must show

– your name in roman letters (such as ordinary printing)

– your photograph.

The examiner might not be able to conduct your test if you are unable to produce one of the documents listed above, and you are unable to satisfy the examiner regarding your identity and licence entitlement.

If the test is not conducted for this reason, you will forfeit your fee.

Legal Requirements of the LGV driving test

Candidates must show that they

- Are competent to drive the vehicle in which the test is being conducted without danger to, and with due consideration for, other persons using the road

- Are competent to drive the vehicle in which the test is being conducted and in particular can:

  i. start the engine

  ii. move off straight ahead and at an angle

  iii. maintain a proper position in relation to a vehicle immediately in front

  iv. overtake and take an appropriate course in relation to other vehicles

  v. turn right and left

  vi. stop within a limited distance, under full control

  vii. stop normally and bring the vehicle to rest in an appropriate part of the road

  viii. drive the vehicle forwards and backwards, and whilst driving the vehicle backwards steer the vehicle along a predetermined course to make it enter a restricted opening and to bring it to rest in a predetermined position

  ix. indicate their intended actions by appropriate signals at appropriate times

  x. act correctly and promptly in response to all signals given by any traffic sign, by any person lawfully directing traffic and any other person using the road.

Preparation: Your vehicle

To avoid wasting your own time and the examiner's, make sure that the vehicle is:

– unladen

– is in the category for which you wish to hold a licence

– does not exceed 60 feet in length (18.28m)

– has the correct L-plates visible to the front and to the rear

– is not being used on a Trade Licence

– has a seat in the cab for the examiner

– has enough fuel not only for the test (at least 20 miles) but also for you to return to base.

– is in a thoroughly roadworthy condition especially:
Stop lamps
Direction Indicators
Lenses/reflectors
Mirrors
Brakes
Tyres
Exhaust/silencer
Windscreen/washer/wipers

Make sure the cab is clean, tidy and free from loose tools, jacks, tyre levers etc. – particularly under the seat which the driving examiner will occupy.

Remember:

You will be asked to carry out a gear-changing exercise during the test unless your vehicle is fitted with automatic transmission.

Some modern vehicles with automated gear shifting systems **may not** be suitable unless the driver is able to select the gears requested by the examiner.

Preliminaries

The examiner will not conduct an eyesight test at the start of your test because you have already met the eyesight and medical requirements before your LGV provisional licence was issued.

Drivers of rigid vehicles (without a drawbar trailer)

No technical questions are asked at the start of your test and the examiner will explain the reverse exercise exercise to you.

Drivers of articulated LGVs

You will be asked questions to test your practical knowledge of safety factors relating to the uncoupling and re-coupling of semi-trailers (including the choice of a safe place to leave an unattended semi-trailer).

Drivers of rigid LGVs with a drawbar trailer

You will also be asked questions to test your **practical** knowledge of safety factors which relate to the uncoupling and re-coupling of drawbar trailers (including the choice of a safe site and methods of securing an unattended drawbar trailer).

Avoid giving answers which suggest that you have learned the order 'parrot fashion'. As part of your training you should be fully familiar with the correct sequence and be able to carry this out in practice.

The reversing exercise

Diagram of manoeuvring area

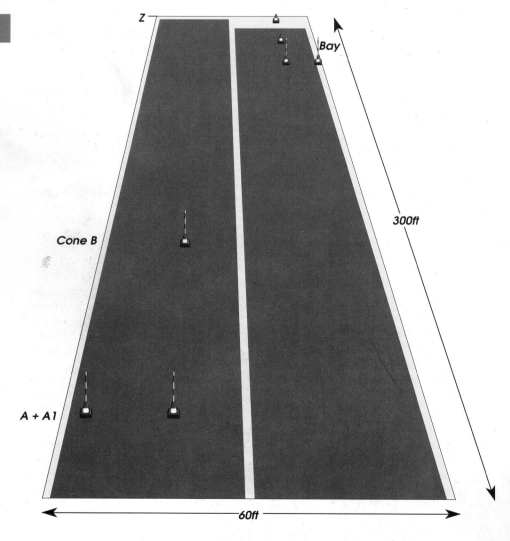

Z to Cone B = 3 × length of vehicle, B to A & A1 = × 2

Reversing exercise

See diagram opposite of the area layout for this exercise.

The exercise is to test your ability to manoeuvre your vehicle in a confined space, avoiding a marker post to enter a clearly defined bay:

- Under control
- With reasonable accuracy
- With effective observation throughout
- Starting at a fixed point (Cones A & A1)
- Reversing *inside* a clearly defined boundary
- Reversing so that the offside of your vehicle clears Cone B

- Stopping with the extreme rear of your vehicle within the solid (yellow - painted) box area at the end of the bay formed by cones.

The examiner will use a diagram of the manoeuvring area to explain the exercise to you.

The manoeuvring area is 300ft long by 60ft wide.

There is a yellow boundary line.

Solo rigid vehicles

Cones 'A' & 'A1' are positioned from the area boundary line.

Articulated vehicles and rigid vehicles + trailer

Cones 'A' & 'A1' are positioned starting 3ft into the area from the boundary line.

Distances A–A1 = $1\frac{1}{2}$ times width of vehicle

A–B = twice the length of vehicle

B–line Z = 3 times length of vehicle

(overall length for the manoeuvre will be 5 times length of the vehicle)

Width of bay will be $1\frac{1}{2}$ times width of vehicle.

Length of bay will be based on the length of the vehicle.

This can be varied at the discretion of the examiner within the range of plus 3ft or minus 6ft.

The precise length of the bay will not be disclosed to the candidate until completing the exercise.

Note: At some centres, there is a steel barrier along part of the boundary.

In exceptional cases vehicles with a long front overhang will start with cones 'A' + 'A1' 3ft into the area.

Part 2 The Large Goods Vehicle Driving Test

Before you start the engine

What the examiner wants to see

Before you start your engine you must always check that

- All doors are properly closed

- Your seat is correctly adjusted and comfortable so that

  - you can reach all controls easily

  - you have good all round vision

- Your driving mirrors are correctly adjusted

- If fitted, your seat belt is fastened, correctly adjusted and comfortable

- The handbrake is on

- The gear lever is in neutral

So develop good habits and practise while you are learning.

After you start the engine

Do not attempt to drive a vehicle fitted with air brakes until the gauges show the correct pressure on the gauges, or if any warning device (a buzzer sounding or a light flashing) is operating.

- You should then apply the appropriate amount of steering lock so that the offside of your vehicle passes clear of 'Cone B' (which also has a marker pole)

- Drive across the area at a reasonable pace in reverse gear by careful co-ordination of the clutch/ accelerator/ footbrake until the rear of your vehicle enters the bay formed by cones (the two cones at the entrance to the bay will also have marker poles).

Note: If you are driving a vehicle with automatic transmission you should make the safety checks which apply to your vehicle.

You are advised to study the operators' handbook.

Faults you should avoid

- Approaching the starting point too fast

- Not driving in a reasonably straight line as you approach

- Stopping beyond the first marker cones 'A' & 'A1'

- Turning the steering wheel incorrectly when starting to reverse either a rigid vehicle + drawbar trailer combination, or an articulated vehicle

- Oversteering so that the front offside wheel travels outside the yellow boundary line of the area (Note: At some LGV test centres, there are steel barriers along the perimeter of the area!)

- Not taking effective observation or misjudging the position of your vehicle so that it comes into contact with (or is about to drive over) 'Cone B' + marker pole

- Not taking effective observation or misjudging the position of your vehicle so that it makes contact with (or is about to drive over) either of the cones + marker poles at the entrance to the bay

- Allowing the rear wheel(s) of your vehicle to ride over the cones marking the boundary of the bay or its boundary line

- Incorrect assessment so that the rear of your vehicle is either short of, or beyond, the yellow box area at the end of the bay (Note: Again, most LGV test centres have steel barriers at the end of this bay!)

Reversing exercise

(contd.)

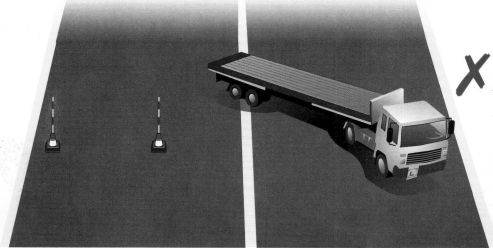

Faults you should avoid

(continued)

- Taking **excessive** steering movements or 'shunts' to complete the manoeuvre — since an overall high standard is expected, only a minimal number of shunts will be accepted

- Driving down the area ahead of a position level with Cones 'A' & 'A1' after you have already begun to reverse.
(You will have gone outside the limits set for your vehicle length i.e. x 5)

- Carrying out the manoeuvre at an excessively slow pace

- Leaving the cab in order to satisfy yourself of the vehicle's position.

You should remember, that, throughout the test, the examiner will be looking for *expert* handling of the controls and a high degree of judgment.

Note: The poles appearing in these illustrations are shown as red and white for clarity. At LGV driving test centres the colours will be black and white.

What you should aim for

- Controlled use of the accelerator/clutch/foot-brake throughout

- Appropriate steering in order to position your vehicle accurately

- Effective observation throughout the exercise (including proper use of the nearside mirror)

- Smooth continuous progress across the area

- Stopping at the positions explained to you by the examiner.

The Braking Exercise

There is no 'Emergency Stop' exercise in the LGV driving test.

For safety reasons the braking exercise takes place on a special manoeuvring area and not on the public roads.

The examiner will be with you in the vehicle for this exercise.

Two marker cones approximately 200 ft (61m) ahead will be pointed out to you.

You should build up the speed of the vehicle to about 20 MPH.

Only when the front of your vehicle passes between the two markers should you apply the brakes.

**Note:
If your vehicle is fitted with a cab which can be tilted forward to make maintenance easier — the examiner will ask you if the cab locking mechanism is secure before getting in.**

If you are not sure — check!

Overall stopping distances

In good conditions a well-maintained goods vehicle in the hands of a competent driver should stop in the following distances from 20 MPH.

Up to 4 tons unladen weight 20 ft.

Up to 6 tons unladen weight 25 ft.

Up to 10 tons unladen weight 35 ft.

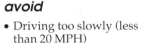

Faults you should avoid

- Driving too slowly (less than 20 MPH)
- Braking too soon (anticipating the marker points)
- Braking too harshly causing skidding
- Depressing the clutch too late (stalling the engine)
- Taking too long to stop.

 ## What you should aim for

Stopping the vehicle

- As quickly as possible
- Under full control
- As safely as possible
- Pulling up in a straight line

The Vehicle Controls

What the test requires

You must show the examiner that you understand the functions of all the controls and can use them

– smoothly

– correctly

– skilfully

– safely

– at the right time

The main controls are

• Accelerator

• Clutch

• Footbrake

• Handbrake

• Steering

• Gears.

You must

– understand what these controls do

– be able to use them competently.

How the examiner will test you

For this aspect of driving there is no special exercise.

The examiner will watch you carefully to see how you use these controls.

Accelerator, clutch, gears, and brakes

Skills you must master

• Balance accelerator and clutch to pull away smoothly

• Accelerate evenly to gain speed

• When stopping the vehicle, press the clutch in just before the vehicle stops

Faults you must avoid

Accelerator

Loud over-revving, so that you alarm or distract other road users — causing excessive engine noise and resulting exhaust fumes.

Clutch

Jerky and uncontrolled use of the clutch when moving off or changing gear.

Note: If your vehicle has automatic transmission, study the details which apply to you.

Gears

Remember that the gears are designed to assist the engine to deliver power under a variety of conditions.

The lowest gears may only be necessary if the vehicle is loaded, or when climbing steep gradients. (Especially if the gearbox has one or more 'crawler' gear positions).

Skills you must master

- Move off in the most suitable gear

- Choose the most appropriate gear for your speed and the road conditions

- Change gear in good time before a hazard or junction

- On gradients it is essential to plan well ahead — whether climbing, or before starting to descend a long hill.

If you leave it until you are either losing or gaining too much speed, you may have difficulty selecting gear and maintaining control.

Modern vehicles may be fitted with sophisticated systems controlled by on-board computers.

These systems sense the load, speed, gradient etc. and select the most appropriate gear for the conditions.

On such systems the driver may only have to ease the accelerator, or depress the clutch pedal, to allow the system to engage the gear required.

The term 'Driving by wire' is often used to describe electronic control systems.

Note: On vehicles fitted with a gearbox with 'high' and 'low' ranges, when you intend to increase speed, it is essential to make sure you have selected the 'high range' position before moving the gear lever across the selector 'gate' — *otherwise you will engage a much lower gear* — with possibly disastrous results.

(See diag. on page 118)

Faults you must avoid

- Taking your eyes off the road when you change gear

- Coasting* with
  - the clutch pedal depressed

or
  - the gear lever in neutral

- Holding on to the gear lever unnecessarily

- Forgetting to move the range selector switch

*Note: This is particularly dangerous in vehicles fitted with air brakes, since the engine-driven compressor will not replace air being exhausted as the brakes are applied, due to the engine only running at 'tick-over' or idling speed.

Typical gearbox layouts

9 The Large Goods Vehicle Driving Test

Footbrake

- Brake in good time
- Brake lightly in most situations
- Brake progressively.

Because most large goods vehicles are equipped with air brake systems, there is frequently no direct relationship between the pressure applied to the pedal and the braking force exerted on the wheels.

This means that good control is needed at all times when braking.

Faults you must avoid

- Braking harshly at all times
- Excessive and prolonged use of the footbrake
- Braking and steering at the same time unless already travelling at low speed

Note: Vehicles equipped with disc brakes permit a technique in which the pressure applied to the brake pedal is proportional to the braking effect applied to the wheels.

Diagram of Air brake system

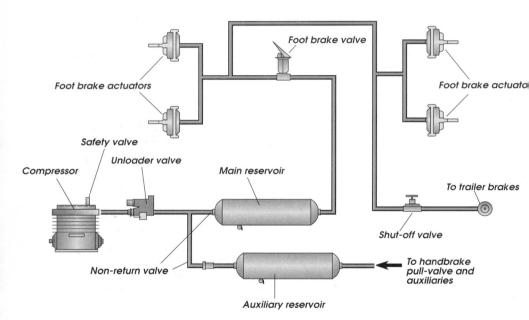

Foot brake valve

Foot brake actuators

Foot brake actuato

Safety valve

Unloader valve

Compressor

Main reservoir

To trailer brakes

Non-return valve

Shut-off valve

To handbrake
pull-valve and
auxiliaries

Auxiliary reservoir

Handbrake

Skills you must master

Know how and when to apply the handbrake

Some modern braking systems will apply a parking brake when the vehicle is brought to a stop by the foot-brake.

The handbrake must be applied when you intend to secure the vehicle before leaving the cab.

Faults you must avoid

- Never apply the handbrake before the vehicle has stopped

- Never try to move off with the handbrake on

Steering

Skills you must master

- Place your hands on the steering wheel in a position which is comfortable and which gives you full control

- Keep your steering movements steady and smooth

- When turning a corner, begin turning the steering wheel at the correct time.

It is particularly important to take the correct path when driving either a long wheelbase rigid vehicle, an articulated LGV, or a rigid vehicle with a drawbar trailer. (See especially road junctions and roundabouts p.140)

Faults you must avoid

- Never turn too early when turning a corner. If you do, you risk

  - cutting the corner when turning right causing the rear wheel(s) to cut across the path of traffic waiting to emerge

  - striking the kerb when turning left

- Never turn too late.

  You could put other road users at risk by

  - swinging wide at left turns

  - overshooting right turns

- Avoid crossing your hands on the steering wheel whenever possible

- Never allow the wheel to spin back after turning

- Avoid resting your arm on the door.

Remember:

The stability of an articulated vehicle can be affected by having to make a 'swan neck' turn after allowing the vehicle to go too far forward at a right turn!

Power assisted steering

Virtually all modern large goods vehicles are equipped with power assisted steering.

This relieves driver effort — especially at low speeds.

When the engine is running, hydraulic pressure is built up in the system so that turning the wheel is comparatively easy.

If the steering becomes 'heavy' you must check for leaks in the hydraulic lines.

Part 2 The Large Goods Vehicle Driving Test

Illustrations of Correct & Incorrect steering

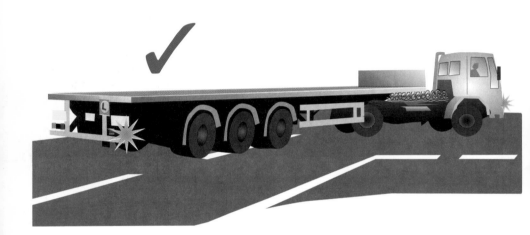

The other controls

You must understand

- The functions of *all* controls and switches which have a bearing on road safety

  For example
  - indicators
  - lights
  - windscreen wipers
  - demisters
- The meaning of gauges or other displays on the instrument panel

Especially
  - air pressure gauge(s)
  - speedometer
  - various warning lights/ buzzers
  - on-board computer displays
  - ABS failure warnings
  - bulb failure warnings
  - gear selection indicators.

Safety checks

You should also be able to

- Carry out routine safety checks
  - oil and coolant levels
  - tyre pressures

- Identify defects especially with
  - steering
  - brakes
  - tyres
  - seat belts
  - lights
  - reflectors
  - horn
  - rear view mirrors
  - speedometer
  - exhaust system
  - direction indicators
  - windscreen, wipers and washers
  - wheel nut security
- Understand the effects which any fault or defect will have on the handling of your vehicle.

The Lost Wheel Syndrome

Research is continuing into the causes of large goods vehicle wheels *(usually the rear nearside wheel[s])* becoming detached even though wheel nut tension was checked and an inspection made before the start of the journey.

It is essential to make sure all wheel nuts are tightened to the specified torque setting.

In some instances, the studs which the wheel nuts thread onto have sheared off despite regular maintenance.

Using the main controls

Moving off

What the test requires

You must be able to move off

- Safely
- Under control
  - on the level
  - from behind a parked vehicle
  - on a hill

    uphill

    and

    downhill.

How the examiner will test you

The examiner will watch your use of the controls each time you move off.

Skills you must master

Use your mirrors

Signal if necessary

Before you move off, look round for

- Other vehicles
- Cyclists
- Pedestrians outside the range of your mirrors.

Move off under control making balanced and safe use of

- Accelerator
- Clutch
- Brakes
- Steering

Use the correct gear.

The Gear Changing Exercise

The gear changing exercise is to allow the examiner to see you engage the lower gears (which you may not otherwise need to use during the test) competently.

The examiner will ask you to pull up at a convenient place to carry out the gear changing exercise (usually at an early stage in the test).

You will be asked to move off in the *lowest* gear and change up to each gear in turn until you reach a gear the examiner considers appropriate for your vehicle.

This will depend on the gearbox layout.

When you have reached the higher gear, the examiner will want to see you change back down into each gear in turn until you reach the lowest gear again.

You will not be asked to select either

– a particular ratio if the vehicle is fitted with a two-speed axle

or

– a particular range if the gearbox has low and high range selection.

You will not be asked to use anything other than the normal gears appropriate to your vehicle.

Faults you must avoid

- Neglecting to check the mirrors before moving off or slowing down
- Jerky use of the accelerator or clutch
- Not starting off in the lowest gear
- Not selecting the next gear in sequence
- Being unable to engage a gear
- Not giving a signal to any following traffic before slowing down.

What you should aim for

- A smooth start in the lowest gear
- Changing up to the next gear as soon as the correct speed is reached

When you reach the gear which has been requested (usually 3rd or 4th) the examiner will ask you to change down when you are ready

- Smooth engagement of the next lower gear — by bringing the speed of the vehicle down by careful use of the footbrake, if necessary
- Returning to the lowest gear when the correct speed is reached.

Throughout this exercise you must

– take effective observation, especially before moving off and slowing down

– give any signal which may be appropriate

– use the controls skilfully to ensure smooth engagement of the gears.

Moving Off on a gradient
Uphill

Faults you must avoid

- Not using the mirrors (nearside and offside)
- Not looking round to check the blind spots
- Not giving a signal when one is required
- Giving any signal which could confuse other road users
- Using insufficient engine 'revs' for the severity of the gradient
- Not coordinating the accelerator, clutch and handbrake with the result that the vehicle
  - stalls
  - rolls backwards
  - surges away.

 What you should aim for

- Taking effective observation before moving off (checking the blind spots in particular)
- Giving a signal (if required) at the correct time
- Using sufficient acceleration, depending on the severity of the gradient
- Moving off smoothly
- Changing up as soon as it is safe to do so.

Moving Off on a gradient
Downhill

Faults you must avoid

- Not using the mirrors (nearside and offside)
- Not looking round to check the blind spots
- Not giving signal when one is required
- Giving any signal which could confuse other road users
- Not co-ordinating the accelerator, clutch and handbrake so that the vehicle
  - stalls
  - surges away

 What you should aim for

- Moving off only when it is safe to do so
- Taking all-round observation (especially the blind spots)
- Giving a signal (if required) at the correct time
- Moving off smoothly by
  - holding the vehicle on the footbrake while releasing the hand-brake until it is safe to move away
  - coordinating the clutch and accelerator
  - moving off in the appropriate gear (depending on the gears available) and the gradient.

Building up speed when it is safe to do so.

Moving off at an angle

When moving out from behind a parked vehicle you must

– take all round observation

– check any blind spots

– give a signal, if necessary

– only move out when it is safe to do so

– not cause any approaching traffic to brake or swerve

– take care (especially with a long vehicle) to move well clear of the parked vehicle

– check your mirrors, especially the nearside, to confirm that you are clear of the parked vehicle.

Faults you must avoid

- Pulling out unsafely
- Causing other road users to stop or alter their course
- Excessive acceleration
- Moving off in too high a gear
- Failing to co-ordinate the controls correctly and stalling the engine
- Swinging excessively wide into the path of oncoming traffic.

Moving off

Using the mirrors

What the test requires

Make sure you use your mirrors effectively

- Before any manoeuvre
- To keep up to date on what is happening behind you.

Check carefully before

- Moving off
- Signalling
- Changing direction
- Turning left or right
- Overtaking or changing lanes
- Increasing speed
- Slowing down or stopping
- Opening your cab door.

Check again in the nearside mirror after

- Passing parked vehicles
- Passing horse riders, motorcyclists, or cyclists
- Passing any pedestrians standing close to the kerb
- Passing any vehicle you have just overtaken — **before** moving back to the left.

How the examiner will test you

For this aspect of driving, there is no special exercise.

The examiner will watch your use of mirrors as you drive.

Faults you must avoid

- Manoeuvring without checking the mirrors first
- Not acting on what you see when you look in the mirrors.

Just looking is not enough!

Skills you must show

- Using the
  Mirrors
  Signal
  Manoeuvre (MSM)

  Position
  Speed
  Look (PSL)
  routine.

Practise

- looking before you signal

- looking and signalling before you act

- Acting sensibly and safely on what you see in the mirrors

- Being aware that the mirrors will not show everything behind you

- Checking your nearside mirror every time after passing

  - parked vehicles

  - vulnerable road users

  - vehicles you have just overtaken.

Always have as good an idea of what is happening behind you as you have of what is going on in front.

Always be aware of the effect your vehicle has on any vulnerable road users you may pass.

Approaching vehicle braking

Giving signals

What the test requires

You must give clear signals in good time so that other road users know what you intend to do next.

This is particularly important with long LGVs because other road users may not understand the position you need to move into

– before turning left

– before turning right

– at roundabouts

– to move off at an angle

– before reversing into an opening.

You must only use the signals shown in The Highway Code.

Any signal you give must help other road users to

– understand what you intend to do next

– take appropriate action.

Always check that you have cancelled an indicator signal as soon as it is safe to do so.

How the examiner will test you

For this aspect of driving, there is no special exercise.

The examiner will watch carefully to see how you use signals in your driving.

Faults you must avoid

• Giving misleading signals

• Giving incorrect signals

• Omitting to cancel signals

• Omitting to signal when necessary

• 'Waving on' pedestrians to cross in front of your vehicle

• Giving signals other than those shown in The Highway Code.

What you should aim for

Giving any signals

• Clearly

• At the appropriate time

• By indicator

• By arm, if necessary.

Acting on traffic signs and signals

What the test requires

You must have a thorough knowledge of traffic signs, signals and road markings, and be able to

– recognise them in good time

– take appropriate action on them.

At the start of the road section of the LGV driving test the examiner will ask you to follow the road ahead, unless traffic signs indicate otherwise — or unless you are asked to turn left or right.

You will be given any instruction to turn in good time — if you are not sure, ask the examiner to repeat the instruction.

Traffic Lights

You must

• Comply with traffic lights

• Approach at such a speed that you can stop, if necessary, under full control

• Only move forward at a green traffic light if

– it is clear for you to do so

– by doing so, your vehicle will not block the junction.

Signals by Authorised persons

You must comply with signals given by

– Police officers

– traffic wardens

– school crossing patrols*

– any authorised person controlling traffic e.g. at road repairs.

Signals given by other road users

You must watch for signals given by other road users and

– react safely

– take appropriate action

– anticipate their actions

– if necessary, give brake lights and/or arm signals to any traffic following your vehicle which may not be able to see the signals given by a road user ahead of you.

This is particularly important when a vehicle or rider ahead is intending to turn right, and the size of your vehicle prevents traffic behind you from seeing their signal.

* Note Sign revision in 1994.

Making normal progress

Remember

The examiner will be looking for a high standard of driving from an experienced driver displaying safe, confident defensive driving techniques.

Under no circumstances should a 'novice' element be evident in your driving.

For this aspect of driving there is no special exercise.

Because you are an experienced driver, and you are expected to drive accordingly, you must

- Select a safe speed to suit road, weather and traffic conditions
- Move away at junctions as soon as it is safe to do so
- Avoid stopping unnecessarily — make progress when conditions permit.

How the examiner will test you

The examiner will watch your driving and will expect to see you

- making reasonable progress where conditions allow
- keeping up with the traffic flow when it is safe and legal to do so
- making positive, safe decisions when you can make progress

Faults you must avoid

You must not

- Drive so slowly that you hinder other traffic
- Be overcautious or hesitant
- Stop when you can see it is obviously clear and safe to go on.

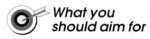 ## What you should aim for

You must be able to

- Drive at the appropriate speed depending on
  - the type of road
  - the traffic conditions
  - the weather conditions and visibility
- Approach all hazards at a safe speed without
  - being unduly cautious
  - holding up following traffic unnecessarily.

Controlling your speed

What the test requires

You must make good progress along the road, taking into consideration

– the type of road

– the volume of traffic

– the weather conditions and the state of the road surface

– the braking characteristics of your vehicle

– speed limits which apply to your vehicle

– any hazards associated with the time of day (school times etc.).

How the examiner will test you

For this aspect of driving there is no special exercise.

The examiner will watch carefully your control of speed as you drive.

Faults you must avoid

• Driving too fast for the

– road

– traffic

– weather

• Exceeding speed limits

• Varying your speed erratically

• Having to brake hard to avoid a situation ahead

• Approaching bends, traffic signals, and any other hazards at too high a speed.

What you should aim for

You must at all times

• Take great care in the use of speed

• Drive at the appropriate speed for the traffic conditions

• Be sure that you can stop safely in the distance you can see to be clear

• Leave a safe separation distance between your vehicle and traffic ahead of you

• Allow extra stopping distance on wet or slippery road surfaces

• Observe speed limits which apply to your vehicle

• Drive defensively and anticipate any hazards which could arise

• Allow for other road users making mistakes.

Keeping a safe separation distance

Always keep a safe separation distance between you and the vehicle in front.

What the test requires

You must always drive at such a speed that you can stop safely in the distance you can see to be clear.

In good weather conditions, leave a gap of at least one metre (or yard) for each MPH of your speed

– or a two second time gap.

In bad conditions leave at least double the distance, or a four second time gap.

In slow-moving congested traffic it may not be practical to leave as much space.

How the examiner will test you

For this aspect of driving there is no special exercise.

The examiner will watch carefully and take account of your

- Use of the MSM/PSL routine

- Anticipation

- Reaction to changing road and traffic conditions

- Handling of the controls.

Faults you must avoid

- Following too closely — 'Tailgating' — on roads carrying traffic at higher speeds

- Braking suddenly

- Swerving to avoid the vehicle in front which may be slowing down or stopping.

What you should aim for

You must

- Be able to judge a safe separation distance between you and the vehicle ahead

- Show correct use of the MSM/PSL routine — especially before reducing speed

- Avoid the need to brake sharply if the vehicle in front slows down or stops

- Take extra care when your view ahead is limited by large vehicles such as other lorries or buses

- Keep a proper separation distance from the vehicle in front in traffic queues.

Watch out for

- Brake lights ahead

- Direction indicators

- Vehicles ahead braking without warning.

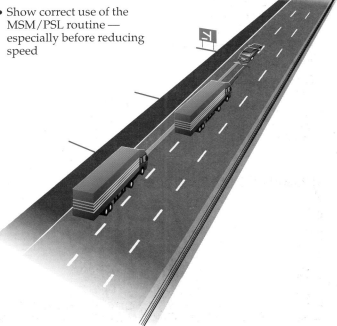

Hazards:
The correct routine

What is a hazard?

When moving

A hazard is any situation which could involve adjusting speed or altering course.

Look well ahead where there are

- Road junctions or roundabouts
- Parked vehicles
- Cyclists or horse riders
- Pedestrian crossings.

By identifying the hazard early enough, you will have time to take the appropriate action.

When stationary

A hazard can be created by the actions of other road users around you.

Watch for

- pedestrians crossing in front
- cyclists or motorcyclists moving up alongside
- drivers edging up on the nearside before you make a left turn
- vehicles pulling up close behind when you intend to reverse.

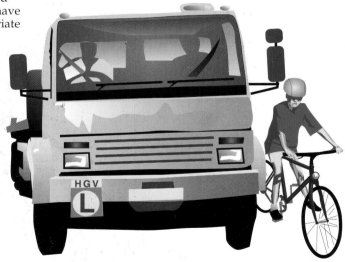

Stay on the alert and watch what is happening around you!

Anticipation and Awareness

When driving in traffic the situation can change from second to second depending on the time of day, the location and the density of traffic.

You can see that some things are obviously going to happen and the skilful driver *anticipates what **might** happen*!

As the driver of a large goods vehicle, you must constantly drive with this sense of awareness and anticipation.

By asking yourself

• What is happening ahead?

• What are other road users doing **or about to do**?

• Do I need to take any action?

   – speed up

   – slow down

   – prepare to stop

   – change direction.

It is essential to be fully alert at all times and constantly scan the road ahead.

By doing this, you will remain in control of both the situation and your vehicle.

In fast-moving traffic you will need to be constantly checking and re-checking the scene around you.

It is essential to recognise well in advance the mistakes other road users may be about to make.

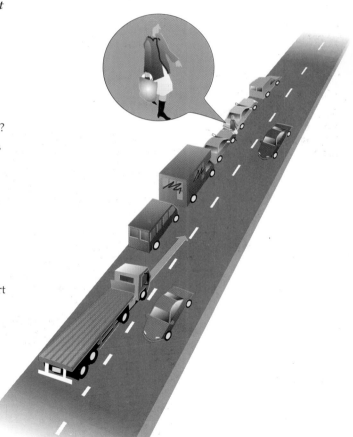

Hazards:
(contd.)

Pedestrians

- Give way to pedestrians when turning from one road into another, or when entering premises such as supermarkets, shops, warehouses etc.

- Take extra care with

  - the young

  - the disabled

  - the elderly.

  They frequently do not realise that you will not be able to stop suddenly!

You must be even more vigilant when driving through shopping areas where there are often large numbers of people waiting to cross, at corners for example.

Drive slowly and considerately when you need to enter any pedestrianised areas to deliver to premises during the hours when unloading or loading is permitted.

Cyclists

Take extra care when

- Crossing cycle lanes

- About to turn left and you can see a cyclist near the rear of your vehicle **or moving up along the nearside!**

- Approaching any children on cycles

- There are gusty wind conditions.

Motorcyclists

Watch for motorcycles

- 'filtering' in slow traffic streams

- moving up along the side of your vehicle (especially the nearside)

- especially when you are about to move out at junctions.

Remember!

'Think once,

Think twice,

Think bike!'

Horse riders and animals

Remember the size and noise of your vehicle can easily unsettle even the best mannered horse

- Give riders as much room as the location permits.

- Avoid the need to 'rev' the engine until you are clear.

- Watch young, possibly inexperienced riders, closely for signs of any difficulty with their mount.

- React in good time to anyone herding animals.

- Look out for warning signs or signals in rural districts.

Avoid

- Sounding the horn aggressively

- Revving the engine, deliberately causing the air brakes to 'hiss', or edging forward when pedestrians are crossing in front of your vehicle

- **Any signs of irritation or aggression towards other road users — especially the more vulnerable!**

Correct road position/ Lane discipline

What the test requires

You should

- Normally keep well to the left

- Keep clear of parked vehicles

- Avoid weaving in and out between parked vehicles

- Position your vehicle correctly for the direction you intend to take

- Obey road markings, especially

  - left/right turn arrows at junctions

  - when approaching roundabouts

  - in one-way streets

  - bus lanes

  - road markings for LGVs approaching arched or narrow bridges with restricted headroom.

How the examiner will test you

For this aspect of driving there is no special exercise.

The examiner will watch carefully to see that you

- Use the MSM/PSL routine

- Select the correct lane in good time.

Faults you must avoid

- Driving too close to the kerb

- Driving too close to the centre of the road

- Changing lanes at the last moment or without good reason

- Hindering other road users by being badly positioned or in the wrong lane

- Straddling lanes or lane markings when it is not necessary for you to do so

- Using the size of your vehicle to block other road users from making progress

- Cutting across the path of other road users in another lane at roundabouts

 ## What you should aim for

You must

- Plan ahead and choose the correct lane in good time

- Use the MSM/PSL routine correctly

- Position your vehicle sensibly — even if there are no lane markings shown

- Always remember, other road users may not understand what you intend to do next.

Watch them carefully and ensure that you signal in good time.

Note: With long LGVs, only straddle lane markings or move over to the left or right when necessary to avoid mounting the kerb or colliding with street furniture such as lamp-posts, traffic signs etc.

Hazards:
(contd.)

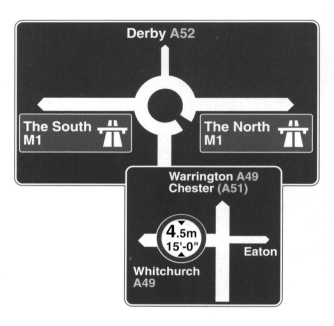

Road Junctions

Because of the size of your vehicle and the difficulties which may arise when manoeuvring, it is essential that at road junctions **you get it right first time!**

Remember!

L . . . LOOK well ahead on approach

A . . . ASSESS conditions at the junction

D . . . DECIDE when it is safe to go

E . . . EMERGE safely at the junction

N . . . NEGOTIATE the hazard (junction) safely

This acronym recognises the difference in techniques between the LGV driver and the car driver and expands the Look Assess Decide Act (LADA) procedure outlined in **The Driving Manual** [HMSO]

What the test requires

You should

- Use the MSM/PSL routine in good time on approach

- Assess the situation correctly, so that you can position the vehicle correctly in order to negotiate the junction safely

- Take as much room as you need *on approach* when driving a long rigid vehicle or a combination of vehicle + trailer

- Take advantage of any improved vision from the LGV cab and stop or proceed as necessary.

- Be aware of any lane markings and the fact that your vehicle may have to occupy part of the lane alongside

- In one-way streets, position as early as it is practicable to so

- Make sure you take **effective** observation before emerging at any road junction.

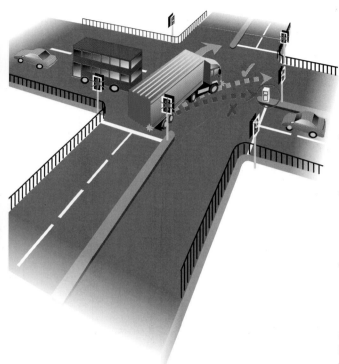

- USE YOUR MIRRORS to observe the rear wheels of your vehicle or trailer **into and out of** the junction

- Assess the speed of oncoming vehicles correctly before crossing or entering roads with fast-moving traffic

- Always allow for the fact that you will need time to build up speed in the new road.

How the examiner will test you

For this aspect of driving, there is no special exercise.

The examiner will watch carefully and take account of your

- Use of the MSM/PSL routine

- Position and speed on approach

- Observation and judgement.

Drivers of long vehicles, articulated LGVs, or rigid LGVs towing a trailer

- When making a left or right turn

  GO FAR ENOUGH FORWARD

  – to see into the road

  – so that the rear/trailer wheels do not mount the kerb

  – so that no part of the vehicle or trailer collides with any bollards or guard-rails.

- If you are crossing a dual carriageway, or turning right on to one, do not move forward unless you can clear the centre reservation safely.

If your vehicle is too long for the gap, wait until it is clear from both sides and there is a safe opportunity to go.

Hazards:
(contd.)

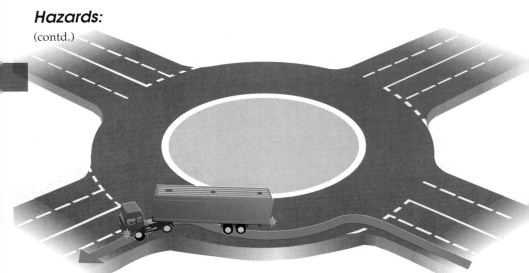

Roundabouts

Roundabouts can vary in size and complexity but the object of all of them is to allow traffic to keep moving wherever possible.

Some roundabouts are so complex that they require traffic lights to control the volume of traffic, whilst at others 'part-time' signals operate at peak periods.

At the majority of roundabouts the approaching traffic is required to give way to the traffic approaching from the right.

However, at some locations the 'Give Way' signs and markings apply to traffic already ON the roundabout. You must be aware of these differences.

It is essential that you plan your approach well in advance and use the MSM/ PSL routine in good time.

It is essential to adopt the appropriate lane depending on the exit you intend to take and the size of your vehicle.

Procedure

Unless lane markings or road signs indicate otherwise:

Turning Left

- Give a left turn signal in good time as you approach

- Approach in the left hand lane (with a long vehicle you may need to take some of the lane on your right — depending how sharp or narrow the exit turn is)

- Adopt a path that ensures your rear wheels/trailer wheels do not mount the kerb

- Give way to traffic approaching from the right — if necessary

- Use the nearside mirror(s) to be sure no cyclists/ motorcyclists are trapped on the nearside

- Continue to signal through the turn

- Look well ahead for traffic islands / bollards in the centre of your exit road which will restrict the width available to you.

Going Ahead
(up to '12 O'clock')

- Approach in the left hand lane unless blocked or clearly marked for 'left turn' only

- Do not give a signal on approach (other than brake lights if you need to reduce speed)

- Try to stay in the lane

  – as far as is possible

  – depending on the length of your vehicle

- Keep checking the mirrors — particularly the nearside one(s)

- Give way to traffic approaching from the right — if necessary

- Indicate left as you pass the exit just before the one you intend to take

- Look well ahead for traffic islands / bollards in the centre of your exit road

- Make sure the rear wheels / trailer wheels do not mount the kerb as you leave the roundabout.

Roundabouts

(cont.)

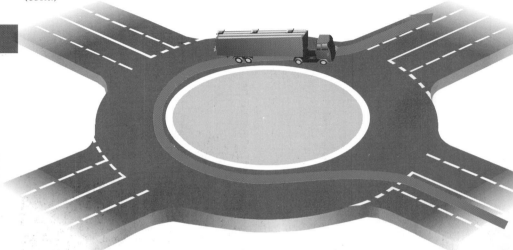

Warning!

Drivers of articulated vehicles or rigid vehicles towing a trailer MUST adjust the speed of the vehicle *in good time* on the approach to roundabouts.

If you attempt to engage a lower gear at too high a speed at the entrance to the roundabout:

The trailer will push the vehicle into the roundabout with subsequent loss of control!

Turning Right or Full circle

(useful to turn LGVs)

- Look well ahead and use the MSM/PSL routine in good time

- With a long vehicle, if there is a choice of two lanes for turning right, use the left hand of the two lanes

- If only one lane is marked for 'right turn' you may have to occupy part of the lane to your left, not only on approach, but also through the roundabout

- Signal right in good time before moving over to the right on approach and watch for any vehicles — especially motorcycles, accelerating up on the offside of your vehicle

Remember

Whichever route you intend to take

- Only enter the roundabout when you are sure it is safe to emerge.

- Keep checking for traffic coming from your right (frequently without signalling correctly!)

- **On no account drive out across the path of any vehicle closely approaching from the right.**

An articulated LGV emerging across an approaching driver's path will present a picture of around 40 feet of steel chassis, side bars, LGV sized wheel(s) and tyre(s) in front of their windscreen!

Not only could the approaching vehicle be travelling at speed, but it is also moving on a curved course and any sudden braking would be likely to send the vehicle into a skid.

- Use the mirrors to observe traffic coming round with you on the near side, and also to check that your rear wheels/trailer wheels are keeping clear of the kerb on the roundabout itself

- Change the signal to left turn as you pass the exit before the one you wish to leave by.

Roundabouts

(cont.)

Lane discipline

- Plan well ahead.
- Look out for traffic signs as you approach.
- Have a clear picture of the exit you need to take.
- Look for the number of exits before yours.
- Either follow the lane markings as far as possible, or select the lane most suitable to the size of your vehicle.

- Use the MSM/PSL routine in good time.
- Signal your intentions clearly and in good time.
- Avoid driving into the roundabout too close to the right hand kerb.

The trailer wheels of an articulated vehicle will almost certainly ride up on to the roundabout unless you pull the steering to the left.

Assess accurately the speed and *intentions* of traffic approaching from the right.

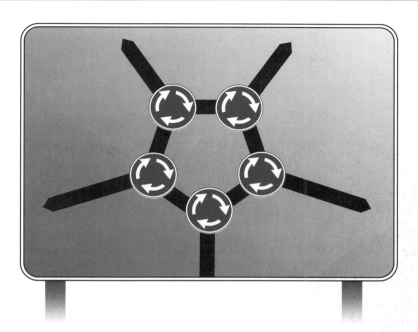

Road surfaces

Roundabouts are junctions where considerable braking and acceleration takes place. The road surface can become slippery and polished, especially in wet weather.

Ensure all braking and speed reduction is done in good time.

If you can see it is clear to enter the roundabout, do so provided you will not cause any traffic from your right to brake or swerve.

Defensive driving

Always watch any vehicle in front when you are about to enter the roundabout.

Make sure it has moved off while you were looking to the right!

Drivers sometimes change their minds at the last moment.

Many rear-end collisions take place in just these circumstances.

Multiple roundabouts

In a number of (usually well-known) locations, complex roundabout systems have been designed which incorporate a mini-roundabout at each exit.

The main thing to remember at such places is that traffic is travelling **in all directions.**

Cyclists and horse riders

It is often safest for cyclists and horse riders to take the outside path when turning right at large roundabouts. Watch for any signals and give them as much room as you safely can.

Hazards:
(contd.)

Mini roundabouts

The same rules apply at mini roundabouts.

Give way to traffic approaching from the right.

Because of the restricted space both entering and leaving these locations, it is essential to keep a constant check on the mirrors.

The rear wheels of a long vehicle or a trailer can easily 'clip' a vehicle waiting to enter the mini-roundabout.

It is most unlikely that LGVs will be able to turn at a mini-roundabout without driving over the marked centre area.

Position your vehicle so that it does not drive over the kerb at the entrance or exit.

Double mini-roundabouts

These require even more care and planning since traffic will often back up from one to the other at busy times.

Make sure that there is room for you to move forward and that, by doing so, your vehicle will not block the whole system.

Although traffic is advised not to carry out 'U' turn manoeuvres at a mini-roundabout, be alert for any oncoming traffic doing so.

Because of the limited space and the comparatively short amount of time it takes to negotiate a mini-roundabout, it is important to give only signals which will help other road users.

Avoid any signals which might confuse.

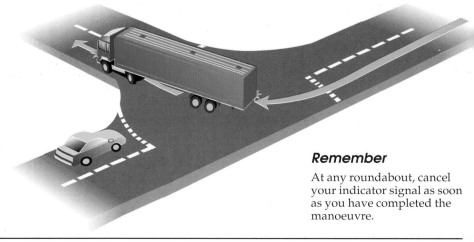

Remember

At any roundabout, cancel your indicator signal as soon as you have completed the manoeuvre.

Overtaking other road users

What the test requires

Before overtaking you must

- Look well ahead for any hazards such as
  - oncoming traffic
  - bends
  - junctions
  - road markings
  - traffic signs
  - the vehicle in front about to overtake
  - any gradient
- Assess the speed of the vehicle you intend to overtake
- Assess the speed differential of the two vehicles (this will indicate how long the manoeuvre could take)
- Allow enough room to overtake safely
- Move out at the proper time
- Avoid the need to 'cut in' on the vehicle you have just overtaken.

How the examiner will test you

For this aspect of driving, there is no special exercise. The examiner will watch carefully and take account of your

- Use of the MSM/PSL routine
- Reactions to road and traffic conditions
- Handling of the controls
- Choice of safe opportunity to overtake.

Faults you must avoid

You must not overtake when

- Your view of the road ahead is not clear
- You would have to exceed the speed limit
- To do so would cause other road users to slow down, stop or swerve
- There are signs or road markings which prohibit overtaking.

 ## What you should aim for

You must be able to assess ALL the factors which will decide if you can or cannot overtake safely such as

- Oncoming traffic
- The type of road (single or dual carriageway)
- The speed of the vehicle ahead
- If you can overtake before reaching any continuous white centre line on your side of the road
- How far ahead the road is clear
- Whether the road will remain clear
- Your mirror check shows that there is traffic behind about to overtake your own vehicle.

Overtake only when you can do so

- Safely
- Legally
- Without causing other road users to slow down or alter course.

Hazards:

(contd.)

Meeting other vehicles and passing stationary vehicles

What the test requires

You must be able to meet and deal with oncoming traffic safely and confidently

Especially

- On narrow roads
- Where there are obstructions such as parked cars
- Where you have to move into the path of oncoming vehicles.

How the examiner will test you

For this aspect of driving there is no special exercise.

The examiner will watch carefully and take account of your

- Use of the MSM/PSL routine
- Reactions to road and traffic conditions
- Handling of the controls.

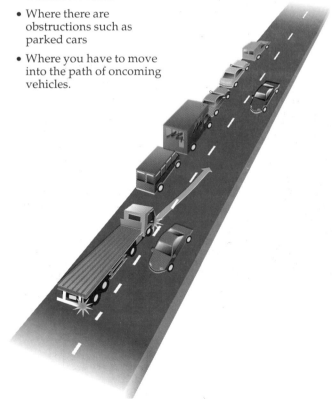

Faults you must avoid

- Causing other vehicles to
  - slow down
  - swerve
  - stop
- Passing dangerously close to parked vehicles
- Using the size of your vehicle to force other road users to give way.

 What you should aim for

You must

- Show sound judgement when meeting oncoming traffic
- Be decisive when stopping and moving off
- Stop in a position which allows you to move out smoothly when the way is clear
- Allow adequate clearance when passing stationary vehicles. If you have to pass close to them — SLOW DOWN!

Be on the alert for

- Doors opening
- Children running out
- Pedestrians stepping out
  - between parked vehicles
  - round the front of buses
- Vehicles pulling out without warning.

Crossing the path of other vehicles

What the test requires

You must be able to cross the path of oncoming traffic safely and with confidence.

You will need to be able to carry out this manoeuvre safely when you intend to

- Turn right at a road junction
- Enter premises on the right hand side of the road.

You should

- Use the MSM/PSL routine on approach
- Position the vehicle correctly as far as possible (the width and type of road and the length of the vehicle will affect this)

- Assess accurately the speed of any approaching traffic
- Wait, if necessary
- Observe the road or entrance you are about to turn into
- Watch for any pedestrians.

How the examiner will test you

For this aspect of driving there is no special exercise.

The examiner will watch carefully and take account of your judgement of oncoming traffic.

Faults you must avoid

- Pulling across the the path of oncoming road users, causing them to
  - slow down
  - swerve
  - stop
- Cutting the corner
- Overshooting the turn so that the front wheels mount the kerb.

What you should aim for

You should

- Make safe and confident decisions when to turn across the path of vehicles approaching from the opposite direction
- Ensure that the road or entrance is clear for you to enter
- Be confident that your vehicle will not endanger any road user waiting to emerge from the right
- Assess accurately whether it is safe to attempt to enter the road or entrance
- Show courtesy and consideration to other road users, especially pedestrians.

Hazards:

(contd.)

Pedestrian Crossings

What the test requires

You must

- Recognise the different types of pedestrian crossing

- Show courtesy and consideration towards pedestrians

- Stop safely when necessary.

Types of Pedestrian Crossing

Controlled

These crossings may be controlled by traffic signals at junctions

or

They may be controlled by

- Police officers

- traffic wardens

- school crossing patrols

Uncontrolled Zebra crossings

These crossings are recognised by

- black and white stripes across the road

- flashing amber beacons at both sides

- zig zag markings on the road on both sides of the crossing

- a row of studs along each edge of the black and white stripes.

Pelican Crossings

These crossings have traffic signals which are actuated by pedestrians pressing a button on the panel at either side of the crossing.

There is a flashing amber phase which is to allow pedestrians who are already on the crossing to continue across in safety.

There are also zig zag lines on each side of the crossing.

There is a stop line at the crossing.

Puffin Crossings

(Pedestrian user-friendly intelligent crossing)

This type of crossing has been installed at a number of selected sites.

They have Infra-red detectors sited so that the 'Red' traffic signal phase may be held until pedestrians have cleared the crossing.

No flashing amber phase is then necessary.

The traffic signals operate in normal sequence.

Toucan Crossings

A limited number of this type of crossing have been installed where there are large numbers of cyclists in areas such as a college or university campus.

Cyclists share the crossing with pedestrians without dismounting.

A green cycle lights when it is safe to cross.

Pedestrian Crossings
(contd.)

How the examiner will test you

For this aspect of driving there is no special exercise.

The examiner will watch carefully to see that you

- Recognise the pedestrian crossing in good time
- Use the MSM/PSL routine
- Stop when necessary.

Faults you must avoid

- Approaching any type of crossing at too high a speed
- Driving on without stopping or showing awareness of waiting pedestrians
- Driving onto or blocking a crossing
- Harassing pedestrians by
  - revving the engine
  - causing unnecessary air brake noise
  - edging forward
  - sounding the horn
- Overtaking within the zig zag lines
- Waving pedestrians to cross.

 ### What you should aim for

At Zebra crossings

You must

- Slow down and stop if there is anyone on the crossing
- Slow down and be prepared to stop if anyone is waiting to cross.

At Pelican crossings

You must

- Stop if the lights are on red
- Give way to any pedestrians crossing if the amber lights are flashing
- Be especially alert
  - near schools
  - at shopping areas
  - when turning at junctions
- Approach all crossings at controlled speed
- Stop safely when necessary
- Only move off when you are sure it is safe to do so.

Pedestrian Crossings

Zebra

Pelican

Toucan

Puffin

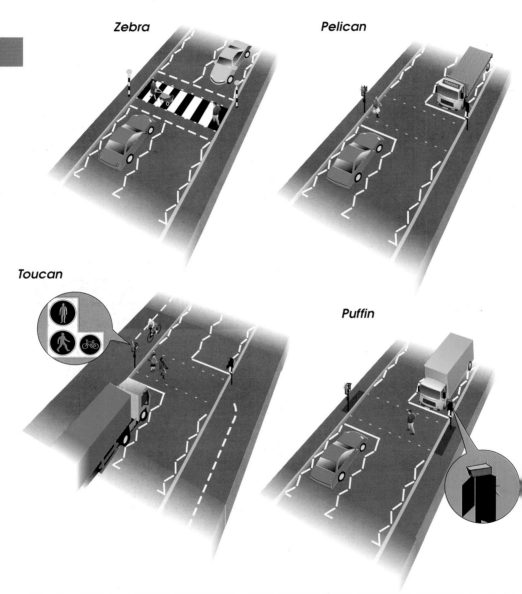

Selecting a safe place to stop

What the test requires

When you make a normal stop you must be able to

- Select a safe place where you will not
  - cause obstruction
  - create a hazard
  - contravene any waiting, stopping or parking restrictions
- Stop reasonably close to the edge of the road.

How the examiner will test you

For this aspect of the test there is no special exercise.

The examiner will watch your driving and take account of your

- Use of the MSM/PSL routine
- Judgement in selecting a safe place to stop.

Faults you must avoid

- Pulling up with insufficient warning to other road users
- Causing danger or inconvenience to any other road users
- Not complying with
  - no waiting
  - no parking
  - no stopping restrictions
- Parking at or outside
  - school entrances
  - fire stations or ambulance stations
  - bus stops
  - pedestrian crossings.

What you should aim for

You must select a safe place to stop by

- Identifying it in good time
- Making proper use of the MSM/PSL routine
- Only stopping where you are allowed to do so
- Not causing an obstruction
- Recognising any road markings or signs indicating any restriction in good time.

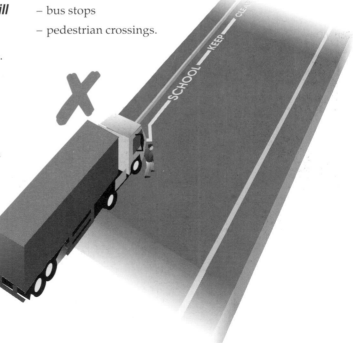

Questions on The Highway Code

At the end of the road section of the driving test you will be asked

- Ten questions on The Highway Code (with particular reference to LGVs)

- Six questions on vehicle safety matters

- To identify six road traffic signs.

For examples of questions on vehicle safety see Part 4 p. 247–9.

SIGNALS BY AUTHORISED PERSONS

STOP

Traffic approaching from behind

Traffic approaching from the front

Traffic approaching from both front and behind

BECKONING TRAFFIC ON

Beckoning on traffic from the front

Beckoning on traffic from the side

Beckoning on traffic from behind

The LGV Driving Test Result

If you pass

You will have demonstrated that you can drive an unladen LGV to the high standard required to obtain the vocational licence.

You will be given

- A Pass Certificate (D10V) and
- A copy of the Driving Test Report (DLV25) which will show any minor faults which have been marked during the test.

You may also be offered a brief oral explanation of any minor faults marked.

This is to help you overcome any minor weaknesses in your driving as you gain experience.

Sign the back of your driving licence and forward it with the Pass Certificate to the Vocational Licence Section DVLC Swansea SA99 1BR as soon as possible (and in any case within TWO years) to obtain FULL LGV licence entitlement on your driving licence.

Developing driving standards

You should aim to raise your standard of driving — especially with experience of driving laden vehicles.

Your trainer should be able to give you further advice.

If you fail

Your driving will not have been to the high standard required to obtain the vocational driving licence.

You will have made mistakes which either did cause, or could have caused, danger on the road.

Your examiner will

- Give you a Statement of Failure including a copy of the Driving Test Report (DLV25A) which will show all the faults marked during the test
- Explain briefly why you have failed.

Study the Driving Test Report and refer to the relevant sections in this book.

Show your copy of the Driving Test Report to your instructor, who will help you to correct the faults.

Your instructor should not concentrate solely on your faults, but will aim to continue to improve all aspects of your driving before you retake the test.

Listen to the advice your instructor gives you and get as much practice as you can.

Note: *Unless you hold a foreign licence it is no longer necessary to complete another Application Form D1.*

Right of Appeal

Although the examiner's decision cannot be altered you have a right to appeal if you consider that your driving test was not conducted according to the regulations.

- If you live in England or Wales you have 6 months after the issue of the Statement of Failure in which to appeal (Magistrates' Courts Act 1952 [Ch.55 part VII, Sectn.104])

- If you live in Scotland you have 21 days in which to appeal (Sheriff Court, Scotland Act of Sederunt (Statutory Appeals) 1981).

See also DSA Complaints Guide for test candidates (Part 4 p. 227).

LGV/PCV Driving Test Report (Form DLV25)

LGV/PCV Driving Test Report

An Executive Agency of the Department of Transport

DRIVING STANDARDS AGENCY

Centre

Date / /

Candidate's full name

Operator or Organisation (where known)

LGV*		Length		Artic*		Make	
PCV*		Width		Draw Bar*		Type	
		Height		Rigid*		Reg Mark	
				Automatic*		Time	

Oral explanation offered Yes ☐ No ☐   Category

Oral explanation accepted Yes ☐ No ☐   *Tick as appropriate

1. Knowledge of uncoupling and re-coupling

2. Knowledge of components affecting safe control

3. Knowledge of the Highway Code

4. Take proper precautions before starting the engine

5. Make proper use of:

accelerator   clutch   gears

footbrake   handbrake   steering

6. Move away:

safely   under control

7. Stop within a limited distance, under control

8. Gears exercise: select appropriate gear correctly

9. Reverse in a restricted space:

under control   with proper observation

10. Make effective use of mirror(s) well before

signalling   changing direction   changing speed

11. Give signals

where necessary   correctly   properly timed

12. (a) Take correct and prompt action on all:

traffic signs   road markings   traffic lights

(b) Take correct and prompt action on all signals by:

traffic controllers   other road users

13. Exercise proper care in the use of speed

14. Follow behind another vehicle at a safe distance

15. Make progress by:
driving at a speed appropriate to the road and traffic conditions
avoiding undue hesitancy

16. Act properly at road junctions with regard to:

speed on approach   observation

position before turning right

position before turning left   cutting right hand corners

17. Deal with other vehicles safely when:

overtaking   meeting   crossing their path

18. Position the vehicle correctly:

during normal driving   exercise lane discipline

19. Allow adequate clearance to stationary vehicles

20. Take appropriate action at pedestrian crossings

21. Select a safe position for normal stops

22. Show awareness and anticipation of the actions of:

other road users

Examiner took action:

verbal   physical

Examiner's name

Examiner's signature

Authorised by the Secretary of State to conduct tests.

DLV25A (1/93)

10. Defensive Driving

Defensive driving for the LGV driver means making allowances not only for the limitations of the vehicle's speed, size and weight, but also for any manoeuvres which could affect the stability of the load.

In addition, an important factor in a lorry driver's defensive driving techniques will involve making allowances for the (genuine) ignorance of other road users who, in most cases, will have very little idea of the problems an LGV driver faces when manoeuvring the vehicle at junctions, roundabouts, entrances or exits for example.

Contents

Defensive Driving

What is defensive driving?

Defensive driving is based on *planning* well ahead, taking effective observation, staying in control and, above all, having a keen sense of anticipation.

Know what others are going to do even before they do it!

Expect the unexpected and avoid being taken by surprise.

Remember! It is not possible for you to brake and/or swerve like lighter, smaller vehicles can.

Develop

– awareness (know what is going on all round you)

– planning (you will have to look even further ahead of you on the motorway)

– anticipating (your experience will soon tell you what other road users are going to do next)

– staying in control (plan **your** actions, avoid being forced into situations by the actions of others).

You will need to drive with

– responsibility

– care

– consideration

– courtesy It is up to **you** to remove the 'cowboy' image from other road users' minds.

With so many pressures on the movement of goods by road, there has never been a more important time to show the public at large just how professional you need to be to drive a modern sophisticated LGV with skill and safety.

Safety above all

By adopting defensive driving techniques you will develop a concern for the safety of all road users in addition to your own safety.

Expect others to make mistakes and to do the wrong thing (*they probably will*).

Make allowances for the vulnerable and also the unpredictable such as

– young children (near crossings, or playing)

– cyclists (especially young ones)

– horse riders (especially obvious 'novices' out with riding instructors)

– more elderly pedestrians (who may be confused or have hearing or sight difficulties, or who have absolutely no idea of the distance needed to stop a laden LGV)

– obviously elderly drivers who may be hesitant or confused; they frequently feel totally intimidated by the presence of an LGV either approaching them, or directly behind them.

– learner drivers (especially at an early stage, who can be very quickly affected by the approach or presence of an LGV particularly when the air brakes go on!)

Control of road space

It is essential that your vehicle is under control at all times.

You must drive it skilfully and plan ahead, so that your vehicle is always travelling at the appropriate speed and in the correct position for the next manoeuvre you need to make.

You should never be in the position of having to do anything hastily. If you are — **you have got it wrong!**

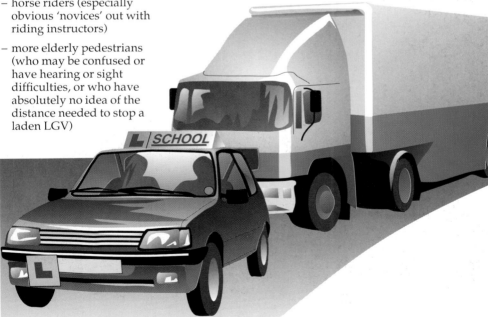

Good examples

Your driving should always be a good example of high standards to others.

Remember your company's name is on the side of your vehicle and avoid the 'cowboy' image mentioned earlier!

By driving with patience and good anticipation, you will avoid

– giving offence to others

– creating hostility

– provoking reactions

– inciting others to drive dangerously.

Driving in competition

Due to the limitations placed on LGVs by load and performance (especially by speed limiters) it may often seem to others that LGV drivers are 'racing' one another.

In reality, it simply takes a long time to get safely past another LGV if the speed differentials are close.

This becomes even more apparent when the road starts to go uphill.

In such cases, the vehicle being overtaken may sometimes prove to have the superior power and the overtaking vehicle has to drop back.

This lack of forward planning may appear to be evidence of racing to the uninitiated.

If another LGV has started to make an overtaking manoeuvre at what was an apparently safe opportunity, but the overtake is now becoming difficult, be prepared to ease your own speed.

It would be safer to allow the other driver to move back to the left.

For this reason, apart from the obvious principle of keeping a safe separation distance from traffic ahead, it is vital NOT to drive in close convoy.

If other vehicles from the same organisation are making the same journey at the same time, DO NOT drive nose-to-tail or, worse still, appear to be jockeying for position with each other along the road.

Remember: Driving in a spirit of competition is the opposite to defensive driving and will eventually lead to increasing the risks, either to your own safety, or perhaps to the safety of some innocent party.

Effective observation

Just looking is not enough!

As the driver of an LGV, in most cases you will have a better view from your driving position than other road users.

However, because of its size and design, an LGV will have more blind spots than many smaller vehicles.

You must use the mirrors frequently *and act upon what you see in them* to assess what road users around you are doing, or are going to do next. You must frequently check down the sides of the vehicle.

Offside

– for overtaking traffic coming up behind, or already alongside

– before signalling

– before changing lanes, overtaking, moving to the right, or before turning right

Nearside

– for cyclists or motorcyclists 'filtering' up the nearside

– for traffic on your left when moving in two or more lanes

– to check when you have passed another road user, pedestrians, or parked vehicles before moving back to the left

– to verify the position of the rear wheels of the vehicle or trailer in relation to the kerb

– before changing lanes, after overtaking, moving closer to the left, leaving roundabouts and before turning left (or right if your vehicle has a long rear overhang).

You must frequently check offside, nearside, offside and so on . . ..

Because of your relatively high seating position, you must also be aware of pedestrians or cyclists who may be *directly* in front of the vehicle out of your normal field of vision, especially

– at pedestrian crossings

– in slow-moving congested traffic.

In addition some LGVs, particularly those with sleeper cabs, give very limited vision to the side.

When intending to move away you may have to wind down the window and look round to be sure it is clear before the vehicle starts to move.

Many modern vehicles are fitted with an additional nearside mirror specifically positioned so that the driver can observe the nearside front wheel in relation to the kerb (or the presence of another road user).

Use it whenever you are pulling in to park alongside the kerb, and to check the vehicle's position when you have to move close to the left in normal driving.

Remember, striking the kerb at speed or wandering on to a verge can seriously deflect the steering, damage the tyre and result in a 'blowout' later.

Part 3 Driving LGVs

Observation at Junctions

Despite having a higher seating position than most drivers there will still be some junctions where your view is restricted by parked vehicles.

If at all possible, try to look through the windows of these vehicles, or watch for reflections in shop windows opposite, if there are any.

If you are still unable to see any oncoming traffic, you will have to ease forward until you can see properly without encroaching too far into the path of approaching traffic.

Remember that some road users are more difficult to see than others — particularly cyclists (who will generally be approaching close to the kerb from the right) and also motorcyclists.

Look

Assess

Decide before you

Emerge to

Negotiate the junction.

Too often the phrase

'Sorry, I didn't see you coming!'

is heard in these situations.

Remember, at junctions,

Think once,

Think twice,

Think bike!

Pedestrians can often act unpredictably at junctions, running out, or even just stepping out oblivious to your presence!

Never make your mind up to go based on one quick glance.

Take in the whole scene before you commit yourself to taking a large and frequently long vehicle out across the path of oncoming traffic.

Zones of vision

As an LGV licence holder your eyesight must be better than the average road user's.

As a skilful driver you must be constantly scanning the road ahead and interpreting what is happening, or what situation is likely to develop.

You should always be aware of what is behind and alongside you. You need to always be using peripheral vision to see changes 'out of the corner of your eye' and react to them

– vehicles about to emerge

– children running out

– pedestrians stepping out.

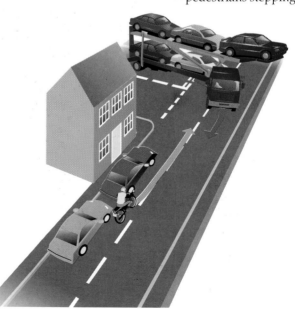

Look for clues!

If you see a cyclist ahead of you glancing round to their right, they are probably going to try to turn right into the next road. Allow for this.

Watch the actions of pedestrians as they approach kerbs.

Elderly people sometimes become confused and change direction suddenly, or even turn back while crossing the road.

Keep a good look out for all horse riders. If the animal starts to behave nervously, allow the rider time **and space** to control their mount.

Remember, the noise of the exhaust from a large goods vehicle can disturb even a normally calm horse.

Planning ahead

Never drive at such a speed that you cannot pull up safely in the distance you can see to be clear, taking into account

– weather conditions

– the road surface

– any load.

This is one rule of safe driving which must not be broken — ever!

Never drive beyond the limits of your vision.

Keep a safe separation distance between you and the vehicle in front.

In reasonable weather conditions leave at least 1 metre (or yard) per MPH of your speed, or a two second time gap.

In poor weather on wet roads you will need to at least *double* the distance and allow at least a four second time gap.

The 'Two Second Rule'

You can check the time gap by watching the vehicle in front pass an object — such as a bridge, pole, sign etc. and then saying to yourself

'Only a fool breaks the two second rule!'

You should not have finished saying this before your vehicle passes the same spot.

If you do —

you are too close!

On some motorways this rule is drawn to drivers' attention by 'chevrons' painted on the road surface.

The instruction

'Keep at least two chevrons from the vehicle ahead'

also appears on a sign at these locations.

In congested traffic moving at slower speeds it may not be practicable to leave as much space, but you will still need to leave enough distance to pull up safely.

If you find another vehicle driving too close behind you, gradually ease your speed to increase any gap between you and a vehicle ahead.

You will then be able to brake more gently and remove the likelihood of the closely-following vehicle running into the rear of your vehicle.

If another vehicle pulls into the safe separation gap you are leaving, ease off your speed to re-open the gap again.

Look well ahead

Look well ahead for stoplights.

On a road with the national speed limit in force, or on the motorway, watch for hazard warning lights flashing to indicate that traffic ahead is slowing down sharply for some reason.

Tailgating

Reference has already been made to the dangerous practice of tailgating when driving at speed *a few feet from the vehicle in front*.

Unfortunately, it is not just car drivers in the right hand lanes on the motorway who commit this offence.

Regrettably, drivers of LGVs can sometimes be seen driving much too close behind another LGV, or a smaller vehicle, often at motorway speeds.

If anything unexpected happens, the ingredients for disaster are already there.

Being aware of other traffic

It is important to know as much about traffic conditions behind you as you do about what is going on ahead.

Before you consider changing direction or altering speed, you must assess how your actions will affect other road users.

Most non-LGV traffic attempting to overtake will normally be catching up to your vehicle at noticeably higher speeds.

Blindspots

It is unlikely that an LGV driver would be able to see much by looking round, especially if the vehicle is fitted with a sleeper cab.

This is all the more reason for being *continually* aware of vehicles just to the rear on either the offside or nearside in the blind spot position.

Quick sideways glance

A quick sideways glance is often helpful — especially

- Before changing lanes on a motorway or dual carriageway

- Before leaving a roundabout

- Where traffic is merging from the right or the left

- When approaching the main carriageway from a motorway slip road.

Using the mirrors

You must use the mirrors well **before** you signal your intention or make any manoeuvre.

For example, before

- Moving away

- Changing direction

- Turning left or right

- Overtaking

- Changing lanes

- Slowing or stopping

- Speeding up

- Opening the cab door.

Mirrors

Must be

- Clean and free from dust and grime

- Properly adjusted to give a clear view behind **(This is especially important when you are transporting an over-sized load which projects over the normal width of the vehicle).**

Looking is not enough!

Whenever you use the mirrors, just looking is not enough. You must **act sensibly** on what you see.

Take note of the speed, behaviour and likely intentions of following traffic.

Take care not to allow your vehicle to 'wander', however slightly, before changing lanes.

An LGV occupies much of the available lane width already, and any move away from a mid lane position may cause an overtaking driver or rider to assume you are starting to pull out into their path!

Traffic signals

By planning well ahead you will ease some of the effort needed to drive an LGV.

By anticipating traffic speeds ahead and easing off the throttle you may often be able to keep your vehicle moving.

This will avoid the need to make a number of gear changes, brake, or come to a stop and apply the handbrake.

Fuel economy should improve, so much so that some companies offer incentives to drivers who turn in good results.

Approaching traffic lights

At many busy road junctions the tarmac is covered in **long, wide, multiple skid marks** indicating that LGV drivers have had to brake hard after approaching at too high a speed.

Signals on Green

- Look well ahead, assess how much traffic is waiting at each side of the junction you are approaching.

- Ask yourself
  - how long has green been showing?
  - am I driving at such a speed that I can stop safely if the signals change?
  - if I have to brake hard, will following traffic be able to stop safely?
  - are there any vehicles waiting to turn across my path?
  - how are the road surface and weather conditions going to affect the vehicle's braking distance?

Signals on Amber

The amber signal means STOP.

You may only continue if

- you have already crossed the stop line
- you are so close to the stop line that to pull up might be unsafe or cause an accident.

Signals on Red

You must, of course, stop at red traffic signals.

However, you may be able to time your approach so that you are able to keep the vehicle moving as the signals change.

This is especially important when driving a laden vehicle uphill to traffic signals.

Signals not working

If you come upon traffic signals which are not working, or there is a sign to show they are out of order, treat the location as you would an unmarked junction *and proceed with great care.*

Signals 'stuck' on Red

To comply with the law you should not pass the red signal unless a police officer directs you to do so.

Sometimes the phasing may have gone out of adjustment and the sequence continues after a longer interval than usual.

Remember, if you drive on, and an accident results, you will have no defence in law.

Traffic Signals

(contd.)

Never attempt to 'beat' any traffic lights

Do not

- Accelerate to try to 'beat' the signals.

Remember the possible effects on the load if you have to suddenly change from accelerating to braking!

- Leave it till the last moment to apply the brakes — harsh braking could result in loss of control.

Remember

The driver of a vehicle travelling across your path may anticipate the lights changing and accelerate forward while the signals are still on red-and-amber.

The combined result of these actions are accidents which could often have easily been avoided.

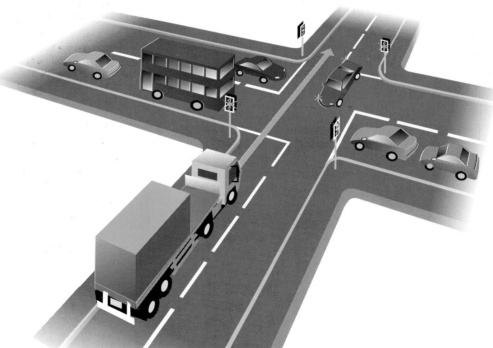

Giving Signals

Signal to

- Warn or inform others of your intentions, especially if this involves a manoeuvre not readily apparent to other road users.

- Help other road users.

Road users include

- Drivers of oncoming vehicles

- Drivers of following vehicles

- Motorcyclists

- Cyclists

- Crossing supervisors

- Police directing traffic

- Pedestrians

- Horse riders.

- Road repair contractors.

Give Signals

- Clearly and in good time

- Which are illustrated in The Highway Code.

Avoid

- Giving any signals which could confuse — especially when intending to pull up just after a road on the left when another road user might misunderstand the meaning of the signal

- Giving unauthorised signals — regardless of how widely you assume they are understood.

This applies to

- **Headlight 'codes'**

- **Alternating indicator signals**

Remember, any signal which does not appear in The Highway Code is not only unauthorised, but can be misleading and is open to misinterpretation by another road user.

Using the horn(s)

There are few instances when you will need to use the horn.

Sound it only if

– you assess that another road user may not be aware of your presence and danger could result

– you need to warn other road users of your presence — at blind bends or a hump back bridge for example.

Using the horn does not

– give you the right of way

– relieve you of the responsibility to drive safely.

Never use the horn as a rebuke or simply to attract attention (unless to avoid an accident)

Do not use the horn

– when stationary

– at night between 23.30hrs and 07.00hrs in a built up area unless there is danger from a moving vehicle.

Avoid any long blasts on the horn which can alarm pedestrians.

If they do not react, they may be deaf!

11. Driving at night

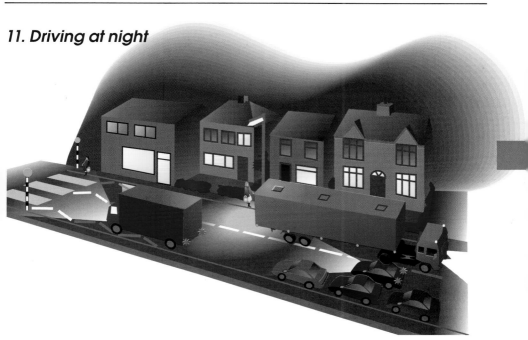

Driving a large goods vehicle at night, often over long distances, calls for additional skills and places added responsibilities on the driver.

Concentration is the keyword, since even a momentary lapse can result in disaster.

Many fatalities have occurred because the driver of a large vehicle either was overcome by fatigue or failed to see a broken–down vehicle without lights until it was too late.

Long journeys at night, particularly motorway routes with little to relieve the monotony, require planning and close attention to proper rest and refreshment stops.

Above all, you must only drive at such a speed that you can stop in the distance you can see to be clear.

In many cases, that is within the distance illuminated by your headlights or by streetlights.

Contents

Your eyesight

As an LGV driver you are required to have a better standard of eyesight than other road users — make sure your night vision matches up to this higher standard.

Have your eyesight checked regularly.

Avoid

– wearing tinted glasses

– using windscreen or window tinting sprays.

Adjusting to darkness

Remember that when you come out from a brightly-lit area (such as a motorway service area) into darkness, your eyes will take a short while to adjust to the different conditions.

Use this time to check and clean your lights, reflectors, lenses and mirrors.

Lighting up time

Regardless of the official lighting up times you should be prepared to switch on whichever vehicle lights are appropriate to the conditions.

If the weather conditions are poor, or it becomes overcast early, don't be afraid to be the first driver to switch on.

See and be seen!

Difficulties when driving at night

The problems related to driving at night are

– much less advance information

– limited lighting (street lights or vehicle lights only)

– the headlights of oncoming vehicles

– shadows created by patchy street lighting

– ineffective lighting on other vehicles, pedal cycles etc.

– dangers created by the onset of fatigue.

Unlit vehicles

Remember that vehicles under 1525 kgs are permitted to park in 30 MPH zones without lights at night time.

Be on the alert when driving in built-up areas — especially when the street lighting is patchy.

Although builders' skips are required to be lit and show reflective plates to oncoming traffic, these are items which are either neglected or the subject of vandalism — watch out for them.

At dawn

Remember that other drivers may also have been driving through the night and may be less alert.

Leave your lights on until you are satisfied that other road users will see you coming.

Remember, it is harder to judge speed and distance correctly in the half light at dusk and dawn.

The colour of some vehicles renders them less easy to see in the half-light conditions.

See and be seen!

By switching your lights on you could avoid another road user stepping, riding or driving out into your path because they had not realised how close your vehicle was or how fast it was travelling.

Lighting

It is essential that all lamps are clean and all bulbs and light units operating correctly.

In addition to the driver being able to see ahead properly it is essential that other road users are able to recognise the size of your vehicle and its direction of travel.

All regulation marker and rear lights must be lit and clear of dirt and obstructions such as ropes, sheets, overhanging projections etc.

If you have permission to move any load at night which projects beyond the normal size of the vehicle all additional marker lights and beacons must be lit.

Although many oversized loads are 'laid-up' in laybys etc. overnight, in certain circumstances the Police Authority responsible for that particular area may consider the load would be more safely moved when there is less traffic on the road — watch for any signals given by the escort with the vehicle.

Auxiliary lighting

LGV drivers must conform to regulations governing the use and fitting of any auxiliary lamps, especially with regard to their mounting height from the road surface.

Remember that high intensity rear fog lights and additional front fog lights must only be used when visibility is less than 100 metres.

It is an offence to use headlights or spotlights whose centres are less than 2 ft from the ground except in poor weather conditions such as mist, fog or falling snow.

If your vehicle is fitted with any additional working lights to assist coupling/uncoupling, loading etc. remember to switch them off when the vehicle is out on the road

Amber beacons are required depending on the load projecting beyond specified limits or the vehicle travelling at slower speeds than normal.

*Drivers are reminded that any light showing to the front should be **white** (or as allowed on some vehicles — yellow) unless they are side marker lights required to be fitted by law to certain longer vehicles.*

Avoid the 'Christmas Tree' effect seen on some vehicles. It can be distracting and confusing to other road users at night.

Remember that any red light used in the cab must **not** show to the front of the vehicle.

Driving in built-up areas

Always use dipped headlights in built-up areas at night.

It helps others to see you and assists you to see if the street lighting varies or is defective.

Be on the alert for

– pedestrians in dark clothing

– joggers

– cyclists (often with poor lighting).

Take extra care when approaching pedestrian crossings — drive at such a speed that you can stop safely if necessary.

Make sure you still obey the speed limits – even if the roads appear to be empty.

Experiments have shown that Ultra-violet lighting can be much more effective than conventional headlight units.

Maintenance work

Remember that essential maintenance work is often carried out at night time.

Be on the alert for diversion signs, obstructions, coned-off sections of road etc. when you are driving at night time.

Street cleansing often takes place in the larger cities — be on the lookout for slow-moving vehicles or pedestrian road sweepers.

Driving in rural areas

If there is no oncoming traffic you should use full beam headlights to see as far ahead as possible.

Dip your lights as soon as you see oncoming traffic to avoid dazzling the oncoming driver or rider.

Be on the alert for pedestrians on the nearside if there is no footpath

Remember

The Highway Code advises pedestrians to walk facing oncoming traffic in these situations.

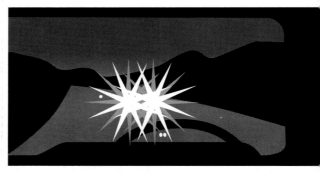

Fatigue and tiredness

Mention has already been made of the dangers of falling asleep at the wheel — remember it need happen for only a second or two to result in loss of control.

The numerous LGVs which roll down embankments from motorways — or wander on to the hard shoulder **with no trace of any skid marks** are usually testimony to the fact that the driver **was** asleep!

Be on your guard

* Avoid driving without a proper rest period

* Keep plenty of cool fresh air moving through the cab

* Avoid allowing the cab to become too warm

* Avoid heavy meals just before setting out

* If you feel your concentration slipping, pull up at the next convenient legal stopping place

* Listen to the radio or a tape (avoid changing tapes while driving)

* Walk around in the fresh air before setting off again after a rest stop.

Fog at night

If there is any possibility of fog developing at night

DO NOT DRIVE!

If the fog becomes so dense that you are unable to go any further safely your vehicle will present a serious hazard to other vehicles.

Because of the difficulties of getting a large goods vehicle off the road in dense fog, it is better not to start out in the first place.

If you start your journey when there is fog about and you are delayed, you will be committing an offence if you exceed the permitted hours of driving for that period because the delay **was** foreseeable!

Overtaking at night

Because LGVs take some considerable time to complete an overtaking manoeuvre, you must only attempt to do so when you can see that it is safe to do so **well ahead**.

This means that, unless you are driving on a dual-carriageway, the opportunities to overtake will be limited.

Unless there is street lighting you will be unable to assess if there are bends, junctions, hills, dead ground etc. which may prevent your seeing an oncoming vehicle.

If you do decide to overtake make sure you can do so without 'cutting in' on the vehicle being overtaken, or causing oncoming vehicles to brake or swerve.

Never close up on the vehicle ahead prior to attempting to overtake.

Separation distance

Avoid driving so close to the vehicle ahead that your lights dazzle the other driver.

Make sure your lights are dipped.

If a vehicle overtakes you, dip your headlights as soon as the vehicle starts to pass you.

Your headlights should fall short of the vehicle in front.

Remember to keep a safe separation distance from the vehicle in front.

If there is no safe opportunity for you to overtake, leave room for smaller, faster vehicles which may be able to overtake you.

Lights on parked vehicles

All large goods vehicles must have lights on when parked on the road at night.

Because a layby is generally within the specified distance from any carriageway, lights are still required!

Unless your vehicle is in an 'off street' parking location, such as a lorry park, it must be clearly lit to comply with the law.

You must park on the left hand side of the road (unless it is safe to park otherwise in a one-way street).

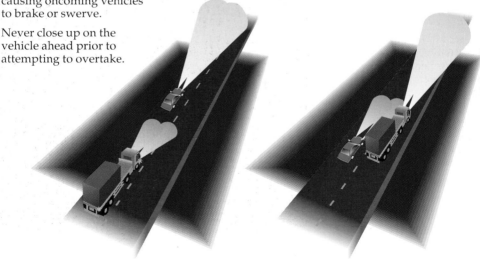

Breakdowns at night

If your vehicle breaks down, try to pull as far to the left as possible.

If you can get off the main carriageway without causing danger or inconvenience to other road users, especially pedestrians do so.

Remember that the weight of an LGV can damage paving stones and damage underground services as a consequence.

Place a warning cone, pyramid, or reflective triangle at least 50 metres (55 yards) behind the vehicle on normal roads or 150 metres (165 yards) on motorways.

Some form of warning is vital if an electrical problem has put the rear lights out of action.

Do not attempt to work on the offside of the vehicle unless protected by a recovery vehicle with flashing amber beacons.

Even then, take great care on roads carrying fast-moving traffic. Many injuries and fatalities have occurred at the scene of what started out as a simple breakdown.

If your vehicle is causing an obstruction and possible danger to other road users, inform the Police as soon as possible.

This is particularly important if your vehicle is carrying any hazardous materials.

If you suspect a mechanical problem, do not be tempted just to 'press on'.

You could end up creating traffic chaos if your vehicle eventually breaks down in a difficult location.

Recovery agencies

If you are engaged in long-distance work especially on 'night trunking', it would be wise to ensure that the vehicle is covered by the services offered by a reputable recovery agency.

The cost of towing or repairing a large goods vehicle could be substantial without the benefit of recovery membership.

Remember that vehicles which break down on the motorway are required to be removed within a specified period for safety reasons.

---

12. Motorway driving

Motorways are statistically the safest road systems in this country.

However, motorway accidents invariably involve a larger number of vehicles travelling at high speeds and usually result in more serious injuries and damage than incidents on normal roads.

Because of the numbers of large goods vehicles using the motorway network's inter-city links, these accidents often involve large goods vehicles.

If everyone who used the motorway drove to the same high standard which *is* required, many of these incidents could be avoided.

An LGV instructor at the DSA Training Establishment at Cardington once said 'Driving on a motorway is like flying in formation — *with strangers!'*

Contents

Motorway Driving

Because of the higher overall speeds and the volume of traffic, conditions can change much more rapidly than on normal roads.

For this reason you need to be

– totally alert

– physically fit

– concentrating.

If you are not you may not be able to react to any sudden change taking place ahead of you.

Regulations

Motorways are subject to specific rules and regulations which **must** be observed by all LGV drivers.

Study The Highway Code sections relating to motorways.

Know, understand and obey the warning signs and signals.

Fitness

Do not drive if

– you are tired

– you are unwell

– you are taking 'flu remedies etc.

– you have emotional worries

– you are unable to concentrate.

Any of these factors will affect your reactions, especially in an emergency.

Rest periods

It is essential that you observe mandatory rest periods in your daily driving schedule.

On long journeys try to plan them to coincide with a break at a motorway service area refreshment stop.

This is especially important at night when a long journey can cause fatigue to set in.

Remember: It is illegal to stop anywhere on the motorway, hard shoulder or slip roads for a rest.

A driver's tiredness is foreseeable and does not constitute an 'emergency'.

If you feel tiredness coming on open the windows, turn the heating down, and get off the motorway at the next junction.

When you get to a service area, have a hot drink, wash your face (to refresh you) and walk round in the fresh air before driving on.

Bear in mind that a substantial meal accompanied by the warmth in the cab, the continual resonance of the engine and long uninterrupted stretches of road especially at night can produce the very conditions you need to avoid!

Falling asleep at the wheel can happen that easily —

Do not let it happen to YOU!

Preparation

Before driving on the motorway, because of the long distances and prolonged higher speeds you must check

• Tyres

All tyres on the vehicle (and any trailer) must be in good condition.

Motorways are strewn with the debris of tyres which have disintegrated under sustained high speed running.

Surveys have shown that: **Many tyres on LGVs are overinflated!**

Make a habit of checking the tyre pressures **regularly**.

Inspect inside as well as the outside visible faces for signs of wear, damage, bulges, separation, exposed cords etc.

Make sure your vehicle has the correct sized wheels fitted (remember smaller diameters will run faster and may overheat on longer journeys).

Ensure that all tyres are suitable for the loads being carried.

Use your mirrors to observe your tyres while you drive.

Check for excessive heat in the tyres when you stop for a break.

It is surprising how many large vehicles can be seen travelling at speed with the driver apparently oblivious to a trailer tyre shredding itself in a cloud of smoke!

• Mirrors

Ensure that all mirrors are properly adjusted to give the best possible view to the rear.

Make sure they are clean.

The simple device of tying a piece of cloth to the mirror bracket works as the air flow causes it to continually 'wipe' the surface.

• Windscreen

All glass must be

– clean

– clear

– free from defects.

Keep all windscreen washer reservoirs topped up, and the jets clear. Make sure all wiper blades are in good condition.

• Instruments

Check all gauges — especially any warning lights — ABS, oil pressure, coolant etc.

Preparation

(Contd.)

• Lights and indicators

All lights must be in working order, even in daylight, to comply with the law.

Make sure all bulbs, headlight units, lenses and reflectors are fitted, clean, and function as intended.

High intensity rear fog lights and marker lights (if fitted) must operate correctly.

Indicator lights must operate and 'flash' within the specified frequency range.

Reversing lights must either automatically operate by the selection of reverse gear, or be switched on from the cab with a warning light to show when they are lit.

• Fuel

Make sure you either have enough fuel on board to complete the journey, or have the facility (cash, agency card, etc.) to refuel at a service area.

• Spray suppression equipment

It is essential that you check all spray suppression equipment fitted to the vehicle and any trailer before setting out — especially if bad weather is expected.

• Oil

The engine operates at sustained high speeds on the motorway so it is vital to check all oil levels before setting out.

Running low can result in costly damage to the engine and could cause a breakdown at a dangerous location.

• Coolant

Because the engine will be running for sustained periods it is essential to check the levels of coolant in the system.

Joining a Motorway

There are three alternatives ways in which traffic can join a motorway.

All these access routes will be clearly signed.

- At a roundabout

The exit from the roundabout will be clearly signed to prevent non-motorway traffic accidentally entering the system.

- A main trunk road becoming a motorway

There will be prominent advance warning signs so that prohibited traffic can leave the main route before the motorway regulations apply.

- At an entry point via a slip road leading to an acceleration lane

Slip roads leading directly on to the motorway will also be clearly signed to prevent prohibited traffic entering the motorway.

Effective observation

Before joining the motorway from a slip road try to assess what traffic conditions are like on the motorway itself.

You may be able to do this from a distance as you approach, or if you have to reach the entry point by means of an overbridge.

Get as much advance information as you can to help you plan your speed on the slip road before reaching the acceleration lane.

You must give way to traffic already on the main carriageway.

Plan your approach to avoid having to stop at the end of the acceleration lane.

Never use the size or speed of your vehicle to force your way on to the motorway.

Use the MSM/PSL routine — a quick sideways glance may be necessary to ensure you assess correctly the speed of any traffic approaching in the nearside lane.

Remember

Look

(for approaching traffic)

Assess

(the speed of any approaching vehicle)

Decide

(when you can safely build up speed)

Emerge

(safely on to the main carriageway)

Negotiate the hazard

(adjust to the speed of traffic already on the motorway).

You must not

- Pull out into the path of traffic in the nearside lane if this would cause it to slow down or swerve

- Drive along the hard shoulder to 'filter' in to the left hand lane.

Note: At a small number of locations traffic merges on to the motorway from the *right* — take extra care in these situations.

Approaching access points

Remember, after passing a motorway exit, there will often be an entrance on to the motorway.

Look well ahead, and if there are several vehicles joining the motorway

– do not try to race them while they are on the acceleration lane

– be prepared to adjust your speed

– move to the next lane if it is safe to do so to allow joining traffic to merge.

Lane discipline

Keep to the left hand lane unless overtaking slower vehicles.

Unless there are road works, and signs indicate otherwise, large goods vehicles are not allowed in the extreme right hand lane on a three or more lane motorway.

On two lane motorways, LGVs are permitted to use the right hand lane for overtaking.

Use the MSM/PSL routine **well before** signalling to move out.

Do not start to pull out and *then* signal!

On a three or four lane motorway make sure you check for any vehicle in the right hand lane(s) which may be about to move back to the left.

Because you are driving a large goods vehicle, most of the traffic coming up behind will be travelling at a much higher speed.

Look well ahead to plan any overtaking manoeuvre — especially in view of the effect a speed limiter will have on the power available to you.

Observe signs showing a crawler lane for LGVs.

This will suggest a long gradual climb ahead.

If a slow-moving oversize load is being escorted, watch for any signal by the police officers in the escort vehicle at the rear.

They may permit you to move into the right hand lane to pass the obstruction.

If a motorway lane merges from the right* (in a few cases only) you should move over to the left as soon as it is safe to do so.

The MSM/PSL routine must be used, with particular emphasis on the nearside mirror.

Note: At these specific locations, no offence is committed if an LGV is initially travelling in the extreme right hand lane.

Separation distance

It is essential that you allow more time for every driving manoeuvre when travelling at motorway speeds.

Allow

- Greater margins than on normal roads
- A safe separation distance

In good conditions

- at least one metre or yard for every MPH
- at least a two second time gap

In poor conditions

- at least **double** the distance
- at least a four second time gap

In snow or icy conditions you must remember the stopping distances can be **ten times** those in normal dry conditions.

Seeing and being seen

Make sure you start out with a clean windscreen, mirrors and windows.

Use the washers, wipers and demisters to keep the screen clear.

In poor conditions, use dipped headlights.

Keep re-assessing traffic conditions around you.

Watch for brake lights or hazard flashers showing the traffic ahead is either stationary or slowing down.

High intensity rear fog lights must only be used when visibility **falls to less than 100 metres.**

They should be switched off when visibility improves, unless fog is patchy and danger still exists.

Motorway signals

Comply with advisory speed limit signs showing on the motorway hazard warning lights matrix.

Watch for any signs indicating a lane closure ahead.

Remember: if RED light signals show on the overhead gantries do not go any further in that lane.

Be on the alert for signals telling you to change lanes and be prepared to leave the motorway.

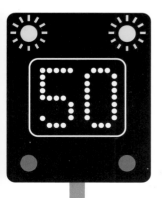

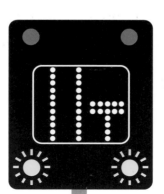

Exiting the motorway

Signs will show

At 1 Mile

– The junction number

– The road number

– '1m'

Half a mile from exit

– The main town or city served by the exit

– The junction number

– The road number

– '¹/₂ m'

300 yds (270 metres) before the exit there will be countdown markers

– 300 yds (270 metres)

– 200 yds (180 metres)

– 100 yds (90 metres)

Remember that the driver of a vehicle travelling at 60 MPH has **60 seconds** from the **1m** sign to the exit!

Even a speed of 50 MPH, there is still only 80 seconds from the 1 mile sign to the actual exit.

Plan well in advance in order to be in the left hand lane in good time.

Large vehicles in the left hand lane may prevent a driver in the second lane from seeing the 1 mile sign, leaving very little time to move to the left safely.

You must use the MSM/PSL routine in good time before changing lanes or signalling.

Assess the speed of traffic ahead in good time in order to avoid overtaking, only to have to pull back in and reduce speed to leave at the next exit.

Do not pull across at the last moment.

Never drive over the white chevrons which divide the slip road from the main carriageway.

Occasionally there are several exits close together, or a service area close to an exit. In such instances, look well ahead and plan your exit in good time.

Watch for other drivers' mistakes — especially those leaving it too late to exit safely.

Traffic queuing

At some locations, traffic can be held up on the slip road.

Look well ahead and be prepared for this.

Do not queue on the hard shoulder!

Note that illuminated signs have been introduced at a number of such locations to give advance warning messages of traffic queuing on the slip road or in the first lane.

Watch out for indicators and hazard warning flashers when traffic is held up ahead.

Use the MSM/PSL routine in good time and move to the second lane if you are not leaving by this exit.

End of the motorway

There are 'End of Motorway Regulations' signs

– at the end of slip roads

– where the road becomes a normal main road.

These remind you that different rules apply to the road you are joining.

Watch for signs advising you of

– speed limits

– dual carriageways

– two-way traffic

– clearways

– motorway link roads

– part-time traffic signals.

Speed leaving the motorway

After driving on the motorway for some time it is easy to become accustomed to the speed, so that when you first leave the motorway, 40 or 45 MPH seems more like 20 MPH.

So

– adjust your driving to the new conditions as soon as possible

– check the speedometer to see the *real* speed.

Reduce speed

Start reducing speed when you are clear of the main carriageway.

Remember that motorway slip or link roads often have sharp curves which need to be taken at lower speeds.

Look well ahead for traffic queuing at a roundabout or traffic signals.

At the end of the motorway be prepared for the change in traffic.

Watch for

– pedestrians

– cyclists etc.

Part 3 Driving LGVs

Weather conditions on motorways

Listen to weather forecasts on the radio.

Because of the higher speeds on motorways it is important to take into account any effects the weather may have on driving conditions.

Rain

Visibility is often reduced by the spray thrown up by numbers of large goods vehicles travelling at speed.

- Use headlights so that other drivers can see you

- Reduce speed when the road surface is wet. You need to be able to pull up in the distance you can see to be clear

- Leave a greater separation gap — remember the four second rule as a minimum

- Make sure all spray suppression equipment fitted to your vehicle is effective

- Take extra care when the surface is still wet after rain — the roads are still slippery even if the sun is out!

Crosswinds

Be aware of the effects strong cross winds can have on other road users.

Watch especially

- after passing motorway bridges

- on elevated exposed sections

- when passing vehicles towing caravans, horse boxes, etc.

If you are driving a high sided vehicle, such as a

- furniture removal van (pantechnicon)

- box van carrying comparatively light merchandise

- curtainside

take notice of warnings for drivers of such vehicles.

Avoid known problem areas such as viaducts, high suspension bridges etc.

Remember that motorcyclists are especially vulnerable to severe cross winds on motorways.

Allow room when overtaking them **and check the nearside mirror as you pass to make sure you have overtaken them safely.**

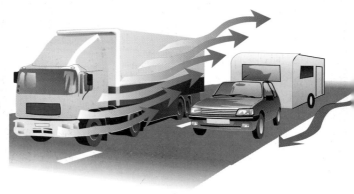

Driving Standards Agency

Ice or frost

In cold weather, especially at night when temperatures can drop suddenly, be on the alert for any feeling of 'lightness' in the steering (not always apparent with power assisted steering) which may suggest frost or ice on the road.

Watch for signs of frost along the hard shoulder.

Remember that the warm cab can isolate you from the real conditions outside.

Motorways which appear wet may in fact be frozen.

There are devices which fix on to the exterior mirror to show when the outside temperature drops below freezing.

Allow up to TEN times the normal distance for braking in such conditions.

All braking must be carried out gently.

Weather conditions on motorways

(Contd.)

Fog

If there is fog on the motorway, you must REDUCE SPEED so that you can pull up in the distance you can see to be clear.

- **Use dipped headlights**

SLOW DOWN

- **Use the rear high intensity fog lights if visibility is less than 100 metres**

STAY BACK

- **Don't speed up again if the fog is patchy — you could run into dense fog again within yards**

SLOW DOWN

- **Don't hang on to the rear lights of the vehicle in front**

STAY BACK

- **Check your speedometer.**

  Fog affects your judgement of speed and distance and you may be travelling faster than you realise!

SLOW DOWN

Multiple pile ups on motorways do not just happen, they are caused by **DRIVERS** who

- Travel too fast
- Drive too close
- Assume there is nothing stopped ahead
- Ignore signals
- Ignore the obvious

YOU CANNOT SEE AHEAD IN FOG!

Even if the motorway matrix signal does not show the word '**Fog**', use the evidence of your own eyes!

Be prepared to leave the motorway, watch for signals.

Be on the alert for accidents ahead and watch for emergency vehicles coming up behind (possibly on the hard shoulder).

Motorway madness

Motorway Madness is used to describe the otherwise unaccountable behaviour of the few irresponsible drivers who insist on driving too fast for the conditions.

It is too late to say afterwards

'I just could not pull up in time to avoid hitting them!'

Police forces have prosecuted drivers after serious multiple accidents and will continue to do so in future until all drivers get the message to

SLOW DOWN IN FOG.

Motorway signals and signs

Motorway signs are larger than normal road signs.

They can be read from greater distances and can help you·to plan well ahead.

Know your intended route and be ready in good time well before reaching the exit you need to use.

Where there are major road works, there may be diversions for LGVs in operation.

Look for the **yellow**

– triangle

– square

– diamond

– circle

symbols, combined with capital route letters

– A

– B

– C

– D etc.

Follow the symbol on the route signs.

Signals

Warning lights show when there are dangers ahead, such as

- Accidents
- Fog
- Icy roads.

Look out for variable message warning signs advising

- Lane closures
- Speed limits
- Hazards
- Standing traffic ahead.

Red light signals

If the RED 'X' signals show on the gantries, do not go beyond the red light in that lane.

- Be ready to comply with any signs to change lanes
- Be ready to leave the motorway
- Observe brake lights or flashing hazard warning lights showing that there is stationary or very slow-moving traffic ahead

REACT IN GOOD TIME.

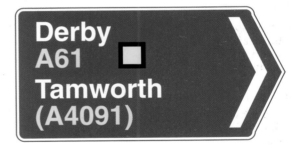

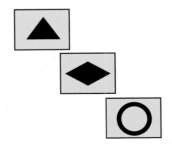

Motorway signals and signs (Contd.)

Contraflows and roadworks

Essential roadworks involving opposite streams of traffic sharing one carriageway are known as contraflow systems.

The object is to permit traffic to continue while repairs or resurfacing take place on the other carriageway or lanes.

Red and white marker posts are used to separate opposite streams of traffic.

The normal white lane marking reflective studs, or cat's eyes, are replaced by temporary yellow/green fluorescent studs.

A 50 MPH MANDATORY speed limit is usually imposed over the stretch affected.

Remember — This means a closing speed of 100 MPH in the event of a collision with an oncoming vehicle also travelling at 50 MPH.

- Concentrate on what is going on ahead.
- Do not let the activity on the other section distract you.
- Do not exceed the speed limits
- Keep a safe separation distance from the vehicle in front
- Look well ahead to avoid the need to brake sharply

- Comply with advance warning signs which indicate lanes which must not be used by LGVs (vehicles over 7.5T prohibited)
- Avoid sudden steering movements or any need to brake sharply
- Do not change lanes if signs tell you to stay in your lane
- Do not speed up until you reach the end of the roadworks and normal motorway speed limits apply again.

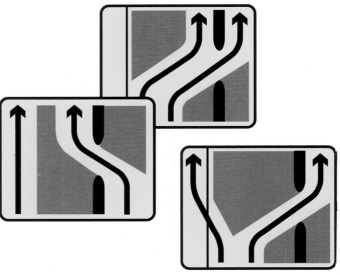

Accidents

Serious accidents can often occur when vehicles cross into the path of the other traffic stream

- Keep your speed down
- Keep your distance
- Stay alert.

Signs

Take notice of advance warning signs (often starting 5 miles before the roadworks).

Get into lane in good time.

Avoid forcing your way in at the last moment.

Drivers of LGVs carrying oversized loads MUST comply with the advance warning notices to either leave the motorway or stop and telephone the Police and wait for an escort through the roadworks.

Breakdowns

If your vehicle breaks down in the roadworks section, remain with the vehicle. These sections of motorway are usually under TV monitoring and a recovery vehicle (free within the roadworks section) will generally soon be with you.

Be alert for broken down vehicles causing obstruction ahead.

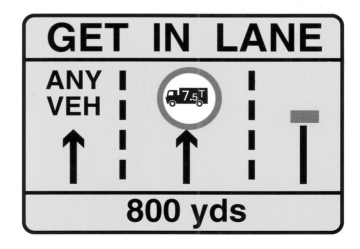

13. All weather driving

Goods need to be delivered 24 hours a day all year round, as the driver of a large goods vehicle, you will need to employ safe driving techniques to ensure that you, your vehicle and the goods in your care arrive safely at their destination with the minimum of delay.

The following section emphasises the skills you will need to achieve this objective during any periods of bad weather.

Training and preparation are vital.

Only the foolish venture out in severe weather conditions without being properly prepared.

It is essential that you take notice of warnings of severe weather — especially high winds, flood risks and, above all, snow or blizzard conditions.

If a large goods vehicle becomes stranded, the road may well be blocked for essential rescue and medical services.

In the case of fog it could result in other vehicles behind colliding with the stranded vehicle.

Contents

Your vehicle

Your vehicle must be in a fit and proper condition at all times.

This means regular safety checks and strict observance of maintenance schedules.

Many cases brought before a Licensing Authority relate to lack of proper routine maintenance.

Tyres

Check tread depth and pattern, examine tyres for cuts, damage, signs of cords visible at the side walls.

Brakes

It is essential that the brakes are operating correctly — especially on wet, icy or snow-covered roads.

Any imbalance would be likely to cause a skid if the brakes are applied on any slippery surface.

Oil and Fuel

Remember to use the correct grades of fuel and oil for extremes of conditions.

Prolonged hot weather will place additional demands on the lubricating oil in engines and turbochargers.

In extremes of cold it would be advisable to use diesel fuel with 'anti-waxing' additives or fuel line heaters to prevent fuel lines freezing up.

In excessively dusty conditions which can be encountered on construction sites, quarries etc., it will be necessary to adhere strictly to schedules relating to filter changes.

Icy weather

Ensure the **whole** of the windscreen is cleared before attempting to move off in frosty conditions.

If you are driving at night time be alert for any drop in temperature which could cause untreated roads to become dangerous.

If the steering feels light you are probably driving on a frozen road surface, so ease the speed as soon as it is safe to do so.

All braking must be gentle and over much longer distances, especially when driving articulated vehicles or those with a trailer.

Remember that you will have to allow more time for the journey because overall speeds will need to be lower.

Keep a safe separation distance from any vehicle ahead. Allow TEN times the normal stopping distance!

Drive defensively and allow for other road users getting into difficulties.

Avoid any sudden braking, steering or acceleration.

Heavy rain

Although many LGVs are fitted with multiple windscreen wipers, you will still need to be able to see clearly ahead.

Make sure the screen is demisted efficiently and that the washer containers are filled with suitable fluid (especially in winter conditions).

Allow more space for braking — **at least** twice as much as in dry conditions.

All braking must be while the vehicle is stable (preferably travelling in a straight line).

Avoid sudden or harsh braking.

Obey advisory speed limit signs on motorways.

Remember that other road users will have even more difficulty seeing when there is heavy rain and spray.

Make sure all spray suppression equipment on the vehicle is secure and operating. Do not use high intensity rear fog lights unless visibility is less than 100 metres.

Construction sites

Remember that heavy rain will turn most construction sites into quagmires.

Take care when driving on off-road gradients, or when getting down from the cab.

If the vehicle is fitted with a switch for locking up the differential mechanism on the drive axle (difflock), engage it.

This will ensure the drive is transmitted to all driven wheels and assist traction by eliminating wheelspin.

Remember to disengage the difflock as soon as you return to normal road surfaces again, otherwise the vehicle may tend to continue in a straight line at the first corner you come to!

It is an offence to deposit mud on the roadway to the extent that it could endanger other road users.

This may involve hosing down the wheels and undergear of your vehicle before it leaves such a site.

Check between double wheels before leaving the site for any large stones or building bricks wedged between the tyres. Such objects can fly out at speed with serious consequences for following traffic.

Snow

Falling snow can reduce visibility dramatically.

Use dipped headlights and reduce speed.

Allow a much greater stopping and separation distance **up to TEN times the stopping distance on dry roads.**

Remember that road markings and traffic signs can become obscured by snow.

Take extra care at junctions.

Deep snow as a result of drifting in high winds can often result in the closure of well-known high level roads.

Take heed of the warnings.

Do not attempt to use such roads if

- **Broadcasts tell LGV drivers to avoid these routes**

- **Warning signs indicate that the road is closed to LGVs (or other traffic)**

- **Severe weather conditions are forecast.**

In prolonged periods of snow, the fixing of snow chains to driven wheels will often prove to be of value.

Some rural roads in exposed places have marker posts at the side of the road which will often give a guide to the depth of the snow.

Remember

A stranded LGV could

- Prevent snow ploughs clearing the route

- Delay emergency vehicles

- Cause other road users to become marooned.

Snow ploughs and gritting vehicles

Keep out of the way of essential maintenance vehicles.

Do not attempt to overtake a snow plough or gritting vehicle.

There is always the possibility of running into deep snow or skidding on an untreated section of roadway.

Keep well back from gritting vehicles.

If these vehicles are out, question whether you should be! Take notice of the fact that adverse weather conditions must either exist or be expected.

Deep snow

If the vehicle becomes stuck in deep snow, engage the 'difflock' (if one is fitted) to regain forward traction.

Remember to switch off as soon as the vehicle is moving and before attempting any turn.

Many vehicles are now required to be fitted with a retarder system.

Engage a manually selected unit before descending snow-covered gradients.

It is often helpful to keep a couple of strong sacks in the cab to put under the drive wheels if the vehicle becomes stuck.

A shovel is often handy if the journey is likely to involve crossing areas where snow is known to be a hazard during the winter.

If the vehicle becomes stuck in snow, use the highest gear which will provide traction and try alternating between reverse and the forward gear until forward motion is possible.

Avoid continual revving in a low gear which will only result in the drive wheels digging an even deeper rut.

Fog

- Do not drive in dense fog if you can postpone the journey

- Avoid driving at all in night-time fog

- Remember it is better to avoid starting a journey which has to be abandoned because it is too dangerous to proceed any further.

The options for finding a safe place to lay-up an LGV off the road in dense fog are limited.

You must not leave any LGV on or near a public road where it would become a danger to other road users.

Do not leave any LGV or trailer without lights where it could be a danger to other road users.

STAY BACK

Keep a safe separation distance from any vehicle ahead.

If you can see the rear lights of a vehicle ahead — you are probably too close to stop in an emergency!

SLOW DOWN

Do not speed up if the fog appears to thin — it could be patchy and you will run into it (or another vehicle) again.

STAY BACK

Do not speed up if a vehicle appears to be close behind.

SLOW DOWN

Keep checking the speedometer to see the true speed — remember fog disorientates and confuses drivers.

STAY BACK

Only overtake if you can be SURE the road ahead is clear — and then only on a dual carriageway.

Just because you have a higher seating position, you may not necessarily be able to see further in fog!

The message is:

SLOW DOWN!

Headlights

Use dipped headlights in any reduced visibility

See and be seen.

Fog lights

Use rear high intensity fog lights and front fog lights when visibility is less than 100 metres.

These must only be capable of operating when the dipped headlights are switched on.

Switch OFF front and rear fog lights when visibility improves above 100 metres — but beware of patchy fog.

Keep all lenses and reflectors clean and ensure all lights are working correctly in poor weather conditions.

Driving in fog

Do not

- Drive too close to the centre of the road

- Confuse centre lines and lane markings

- Drive without using headlights

- Speed up because the fog appears to thin

- Use full beam when following another vehicle — the shadows will make it difficult for the driver ahead to see.

Remember

A large vehicle travelling ahead of you may temporarily displace some of the fog — making it appear clearer than it is.

In a larger vehicle you may be able to see ahead over some low-lying fog.

Do not speed up in case there are smaller vehicles in front which may be hidden from your view.

Reflective studs

The colours of reflective studs or 'cats' eyes' are

- Red on the left hand edge of carriageways

- White to indicate lane markings

- Green at slip roads and laybys

Amber reflectors indicate the right hand edge of the carriageway and a centre reservation

On some rural roads, there are black and white marker posts with red reflectors on the left hand side, and white reflectors on the right hand side of the road.

The continuous white line between the left hand lane and the hard shoulder (and at the left hand edge of some trunk roads) incorporates a 'rumble' strip which produces a vibration designed to warn drivers when the vehicle crosses this line.

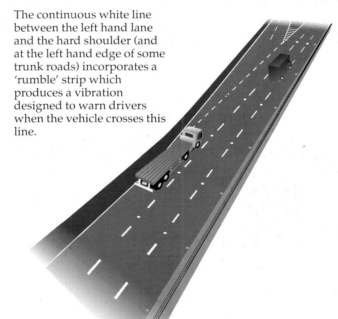

High winds

In severe weather conditions, it will pay you to plan your journey in advance by listening to, watching or reading the weather forecast well ahead (often 24 hrs) if you are the driver of

– a high sided vehicle (removal vans, long wheelbase box vans etc.)

– a vehicle with curtainside body or trailer

– a vehicle transporting portable buildings etc. with large flat surfaces susceptible to wind pressures

– a vehicle towing a horse box

– an unladen van of any description.

If your route takes in any locations which are frequently subjected to high winds such as

• High level bridges

• High level roads

• Exposed viaducts

• Exposed stretches of motorway

Take notice of the advance warnings — always remember that

• The route may be closed to certain LGVs

• There may be additional delays due to lane closures (this is done on high level bridges to create empty 'buffer' lanes when vehicles are blown off course)

• You may need to use an alternative route

• If you ignore the warnings, your vehicle and its load could be lost **and** you could place yourself and other road users in danger.

Bear in mind that ferry sailings are likely to be affected by gale force winds resulting in delays or cancellation.

Watch for signs indicating high winds.

Beware of fallen trees or damaged branches which could hit your vehicle.

Effects on other road users

In such conditions, other road users are likely to be affected

– when overtaking your vehicle

– when you overtake them.

So check the nearside mirror(s) to ensure that they still have control of their vehicle after you have overtaken.

Be on the alert for vehicles or motorcyclists 'wandering' into your lane.

Again, do not ignore warnings of severe winds — if your vehicle is blown over, you could delay the emergency services from reaching a more serious incident.

14. Accidents and Breakdowns

One definition describes an accident as something which happens by chance and chance as being 'risk', 'venture', 'fortune' or 'luck'.

Road traffic accidents (RTAs) frequently occur when road users take risks or 'push their luck'!

By making defensive driving the cornerstone of your driving skill you will remove much of the risk element.

If you do become involved or have to stop at the scene of an RTA, this section outlines the action you should take to prevent further injury or harm to other road users.

Breakdowns

Even in the best regulated systems breakdowns will sometimes occur.

This section also gives a brief outline of the correct procedures to adopt to ensure your safety and the safety of other road users.

Contents

Road Traffic Accidents

If your vehicle is involved in a road traffic accident

YOU MUST STOP

it is an offence not to do so.

The problem with large goods vehicles is that the driver is sometimes unaware that an incident has taken place, especially at night time.

When driving, you must at all times anticipate the actions of other road users around you.

It is important to recognise the effects your vehicle can have on the more vulnerable road users such as cyclists, pedestrians and motor cyclists.

A large goods vehicle can create a vacuum effect when travelling at speed.

Pedestrians near the edge of the kerb and cyclists are especially vulnerable to the danger of being drawn under the wheels of your vehicle or any trailer.

Remember, by

- Concentrating
- Staying alert
- Being fully fit
- Observing the changes in traffic conditions
- Planning well ahead
- Driving at a safe speed to suit the road, traffic and weather conditions
- Keeping your vehicle in good mechanical condition
- Ensuring the load is securely stowed
- Driving safely and sensibly
- Avoiding the need to rush
- Never acting hastily

you will remove most of the potential causes of accidents from your own driving.

The scene at a serious accident involving a large goods vehicle and a bus carrying school children.

At an accident scene

If you are the first, or among one of the first, to arrive at the scene of an RTA — your actions could be vital.

It is essential to

- Warn other traffic approaching the scene by means of hazard warning flashers, beacons, cones, advance warning triangles etc.

- Reduce the risk of fire by making sure all naked lights, cigarettes etc. are extinguished

- If there is injury, or danger to other road users, make sure someone telephones 999 giving details of the incident

- If the injured persons can be protected from any danger from traffic, hazardous materials etc. it may well be best to keep them still until the emergency services arrive

- Be especially careful about moving any casualties — incorrect handling could cause more injury or even prove fatal

- Move any apparently uninjured persons away from the vehicles to a place of safety

- If anyone is unconscious, be prepared to give first aid as described on page 214

- Remember that a person who may appear to have no injuries may be suffering from the effects of shock

- Keep casualties warm but give nothing to eat or drink until medical help arrives

- When an ambulance arrives, give the FACTS to the crew (not assumptions etc.).

Accidents on the motorway

Because of the higher speeds and increased danger of an accident becoming a serious incident it is essential to inform the motorway Police and emergency services as quickly as possible.

- Use the nearest emergency telephone if no mobile telephone is available

- Do not cross the carriageway to get to an emergency telephone

- Try to warn oncoming traffic if possible without placing yourself in danger

- Move any uninjured people well away from the main carriageway on to an embankment etc.

- Be on the alert for emergency vehicles approaching the incident along the hard shoulder.

Hazardous materials

If a road traffic accident involves a vehicle displaying either a hazard warning information plate or plain orange rectangle

- Give the emergency services as much information about the labels and any other markings as possible

- If there is an emergency telephone number on the plate of a vehicle involved in any spillage, contact the number given

- Keep well away from such a vehicle unless you have to save life

- Even then, you must beware of any dangerous liquids, dusts, vapours — no matter how small the concentration may appear to be

- Remember, people have received extremely serious injury as a result of a fine spray of corrosive fluid leaking from a pinhole puncture in a tank vessel.

If you are involved in an accident

- **STOP!** It is an offence not to do so
- You must inform the Police **as soon as possible, and in any case within 24 hours**
  - if there is injury to any person not in your vehicle
  - if damage is caused to another vehicle or property, and the owner is either not present, or cannot be easily found
  - if the accident involves any of the animals specified in law
- Produce your insurance documents, driving licence, and give your name and address to any Police officer who may require it
- Give these details to any other road user involved in the accident if they have reasonable grounds to request them

- If you are unable to produce your documents at the time, you must report the accident to the Police as soon as possible, and in any case, within 24 hours.

The Police may require you to produce your documents within seven days at a Police station of your choice **or as soon as is reasonably possible if you are on a journey which takes you out of the country at the time and you cannot produce the documents within the seven days specified**.

- Exchange particulars with any other driver or road user involved in the RTA
- Obtain names and addresses of any witnesses who SAW the accident

- Make a note of
  - the time
  - the location
  - street names
  - vehicle registration numbers
  - weather conditions
  - lighting (if applicable)
  - any road signs or road markings
  - road conditions
  - damage to vehicles or property
  - traffic lights (colour at the time)
  - any indicator signals or warning (horn)
  - any statements made by the other party or parties
  - any skid marks, debris, etc.

Important note

See page 33 for action to be taken if the incident involves impact with any railway bridge.

First Aid on the road

Regulations require many large goods vehicles carrying chemicals etc. to carry First Aid equipment.

Even if you do not have to carry a kit by law, it is sensible for every LGV driver to have a First Aid kit available.

Learn First Aid

There are courses available from

- The St. John Ambulance Association and Brigade
- St. Andrew's Ambulance Association
- The British Red Cross Society

Get first aid training.

Someday it could save a life!

The following information may be of assistance.

Accident victims

Unconscious

It is vital that action is taken within the first three minutes of an incident if any casualty is to be saved.

(Remember: A B C)

- **A**irway must be cleared of any obstruction and kept open
- **B**reathing must be established and maintained
- **C**irculation must be maintained and severe bleeding stopped

Breathing stopped

Get breathing started again

- Remove any obstruction such as false teeth, chewing gum etc.
- Keep the victim's head tilted backwards

Breathing and colour should improve.

If not

- Place a clean piece of material, such as a handkerchief, over the injured person's mouth
- Pinch the casualty's nostrils together, and blow into the mouth until the chest rises
- Let your mouth surround the mouth and nose of small children and babies and blow **very gently**
- Take your mouth away and wait for the chest to fall
- Withdraw, then repeat regularly once every four seconds until breathing restarts and the casualty can breathe without help.

Do not give up!

Never assume someone is dead.

Keep giving mouth to mouth resuscitation until medical help is available.

Unconscious and breathing

Warning: If you suspect a head injury avoid moving the casualty if at all possible until medical help is available.

Only move the casualty if they are in danger of further injury.

If breathing becomes difficult or stops, employ the treatment described above.

It is vital to obtain skilled medical help as soon as possible.

Make sure someone dials 999

Bleeding

Put firm pressure on the wound without pressing on anything which may be caught in, or project from, the wound.

Use the cleanest material available.

Secure a pad with a bandage or length of cloth.

If a limb is bleeding but not broken, raise it to lessen the flow of blood.

Remember that any restriction of blood circulation for more than a short period of time may result in long term injury.

Dealing with shock

The effects of trauma may not be immediately obvious.

However, prompt treatment can help to minimise the effects of shock.

- **Do not give anything to eat or drink** until medical advice is available
- Reassure the patient confidently and keep checking them.
- Keep any casualties warm and make them as comfortable as possible
- Try to calm any hysterical person by talking to them in firm quiet tones.
- Make sure they do not run into further danger from traffic
- Avoid leaving anyone alone
- Avoid unnecessary movement
- If a casualty **does** need to be moved for safety reasons, take care to avoid more serious injury when deciding to place them in the recovery position.

Warning: Do not attempt to remove a safety helmet unless absolutely essential — otherwise an injured motorcyclist could sustain more serious injuries.

Electric shock

Remember! A vehicle can
come into contact with
overhead cables or electrical
supplies to traffic bollards,
traffic lights or street
lighting standards as a result
of an accident.

Make a quick check before
attempting to pull someone
from a vehicle in such cases.

Do not touch any person
who is obviously in contact
with a live electric cable
unless you can use some
non-conducting item such as
a dry sweeping brush,
length of wood etc.

Fire

Fire can occur on large goods vehicles in a number of locations

- Engine
- Load
- Transmission
- Tyres
- Fuel system
- Electrical circuits.

IT IS VITAL THAT ANY OUTBREAK IS TACKLED WITHOUT DELAY

A vehicle and its load can be destroyed by fire within an alarmingly short space of time.

If danger to others is to be avoided, it is essential to

- Stop as quickly and safely as possible if fire is suspected or discovered
- Get all persons out of the vehicle
- Either dial 999 or get someone else to do it **immediately**
- If possible, tackle the source with a **suitable** fire extinguisher.

Hazardous materials

If the fire involves a vehicle carrying hazardous materials

- The driver must have received training in dealing with such an emergency
- Specialist fire fighting equipment must be available on the vehicle
- Keep all members of the public and other traffic well away from the incident
- If at all possible, isolate the vehicle to reduce danger to the surrounding area

- Ensure someone contacts the emergency telephone number given on either the hazard warning plate or the load documents without delay
- warn approaching traffic.

Remember:

**STAY CALM
REACT PROMPTLY!**

Fire Extinguishers

You must be able to recognise the various types of extinguisher and know which fires they are intended to tackle.

It is dangerous to tackle a fuel fire with a water-type 'soda-acid' fire extinguisher since this may not only spread the fire further, but may cause a violent explosion.

Extinguishers which are intended to smother the source of the fire by the action of either an inert gas or a dry powder are illustrated on page 219 opposite.

Try to isolate the source of the fire.

Do not open an engine housing etc. wide if you can direct the extinguisher though a small gap.

Avoid operating a fire extinguisher in a confined space.

If at all possible,

• Disconnect electrical leads

• Cut off fuel supply.

Note: Vehicles carrying high risk materials are subject to detailed emergency procedures which must be followed to the letter.

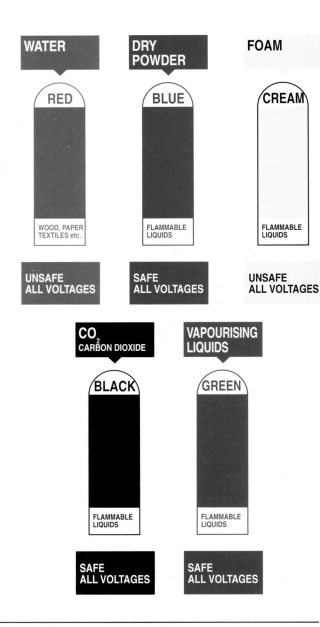

WATER — RED — WOOD, PAPER TEXTILES etc. — UNSAFE ALL VOLTAGES

DRY POWDER — BLUE — FLAMMABLE LIQUIDS — SAFE ALL VOLTAGES

FOAM — CREAM — FLAMMABLE LIQUIDS — UNSAFE ALL VOLTAGES

CO_2 CARBON DIOXIDE — BLACK — FLAMMABLE LIQUIDS — SAFE ALL VOLTAGES

VAPOURISING LIQUIDS — GREEN — FLAMMABLE LIQUIDS — SAFE ALL VOLTAGES

Types of fire extinguisher in common use — and their purpose.

Breakdowns

Many LGV breakdowns involve tyre failures or 'blowouts'.

Apart from these being dangerous in themselves by causing loss of control, the resulting debris presents a common hazard to other road users.

Front wheel 'blowouts'

A sudden deflation of the front tyre on an LGV can result in loss of steering control

- Keep firm hold of the steering wheel

- You should always be aware if there is anything on your nearside

- Signal to move to the left

- Try to steer a steady course to the nearside (or hard shoulder on the motorway)

- Reduce speed gradually — **avoid** any harsh braking

- Try to bring the vehicle to rest **under control** as far to the left as possible

- If necessary, place a warning triangle, cones etc., behind the vehicle and operate the hazard warning flashers if it is causing an obstruction.

By avoiding sharp braking and excessive steering movements, you should be able to bring the vehicle to rest safely without skidding.

Rear wheel 'blowouts'

If a rear tyre on either the vehicle or a trailer deflates the effects may not be quite so severe.

On a large vehicle this may not be immediately obvious to you if it is a multi-axle trailer.

Keep the trailer under observation at all times during a journey.

Breakdowns on the motorway

- Try to get the vehicle as far to the left as possible

- Do not attempt even minor repairs on the motorway

- Place a warning triangle or cones 150 metres behind the vehicle

- Operate the hazard warning flashers on the vehicle

- Make sure the vehicle lights are on at night time unless an electrical fault prevents you doing so

- Use the emergency telephone to notify the motorway control centre who will contact a recovery contractor

- The location of the nearest telephone will be indicated by the direction of the arrow on the marker posts at intervals along the edge of the hard shoulder

- Do not cross the carriageway or any slip road to reach a telephone

Emergency telephones

The motorway emergency telephones are free.

You will be connected directly to the motorway Police control centre.

Face the oncoming traffic while using the phone.

Objects or part of a load falling on the motorway

If an object or part of any load falls on to the motorway from either your vehicle or any other

- **Do not attempt to recover it yourself**

- Use the nearest emergency telephone to call the Police **without delay**

- Do not stand on the carriageway to warn oncoming traffic.

Additional Information

Part 4 Additional Information

Retesting disqualified drivers

Tougher penalties now exist for anyone convicted of certain dangerous driving offences.

If a driver is convicted of a dangerous driving offence they would lose all LGV entitlement.

The decision as to whether they would be required to undergo an extended motor car test before they are allowed to drive an LGV again rests with the Licensing Authority.

Important Note:

You should remember that a Large Goods Vehicle driving licence *cannot* stand on its own.

You *must* also possess a valid full driving licence for Category B (i.e. motor car licence).

If you lose your Category B licence entitlement you lose your LGV Licence.

Applying for a Retest

A person subject to a Category B retest can apply for a provisional licence at the end of the period of disqualification.

The normal rules for provisional licence holders apply

• The driver must be supervised by a person who is at least 21 years of age and who has held (and still holds) a full licence for the category of vehicle being driven for at least three years

• L-plates must be displayed to the front and rear of the vehicle

• Driving on motorways is not allowed

• LGVs may not be driven on a provisional motor car (Category B) licence.

Note: There is no extended LGV Driving Test which is already of $1^1/_2$ hours duration.

DSA Service Standards For Test Candidates

The Driving Standards Agency is committed to providing the following standard of service for test candidates:

- The national average waiting time for a car test will be no more than 6 weeks

- Test appointments will be available within 10 weeks at any permanent test centre

- The national average waiting time for a motorcycle, lorry or bus test will be no more than 4 weeks

- Unsuccessful candidates will be offered an oral and written explanation of the reasons for their test result by the examiner at the end of their test

- Test appointment notifications will be issued within 7 working days of receipt of a correctly completed application form and appropriate fee

- 90% of telephone calls to booking offices will be answered within 1 minute

- Refund of test fees will be issued within 3 weeks of a valid claim with supporting information

- All letters to DSA, including complaints, will be answered within 10 working days.

DSA Compensation Code For Test Candidates

The DSA will normally refund the fee, or give a free re-booking, in the following cases:

- Where the appointments are cancelled by us — for any reason

- Where appointments are cancelled by the candidate, who gives at least 10 clear working days' notice for car and motorcycle tests, **or 5 clear working days' notice for lorry and bus tests**

- Where the candidate keeps the test appointment, but the test does not take place, or is not completed for reasons not attributable to him/her — nor to any vehicle provided by him/her for the test. In addition we will normally consider reasonable claims from the candidate for financial loss, or expenditure unavoidably and directly incurred by him/her, as a result of DSA cancelling the test at short notice (other than for reasons of bad weather).

For example, we will normally consider a claim for the commercial hire of the vehicle for the test.

Applications should be made to the Regional Office where the test was booked.

This Compensation Code does not affect your existing legal rights.

DSA Complaints Guide For Test Candidates

The Driving Standards Agency (DSA) aims to give our customers the best possible service.

Please tell us:

- When we have done well

- When you are not satisfied

Your comments can help us to improve the service we offer.

If you have any questions about how your test was carried out please contact the local Supervising Examiner whose address is displayed in your local Driving Test Centre.

If you are dissatisfied with the reply or you wish to comment on other matters you can write to the Regional Manager (please see the list of Regional Offices on page 228).

If your concern relates to Approved Driving Instructors you should write to:

The Registrar of Approved Driving Instructors
Driving Standards Agency
Stanley House
Talbot Street
Nottingham NG1 5GU

Finally you can write to

The Chief Executive
Driving Standards Agency
Stanley House
Talbot Street
Nottingham NG1 5GU.

None of this removes your rights to take your complaint to:

- Your Member of Parliament, who may decide to raise your case personally with the DSA Chief Executive, the Minister, or the Parliamentary Commissioner for Administration (the Ombudsman)

- A Magistrate's Court (in Scotland to the Sheriff in whose Jurisdiction you live) if you have grounds for believing that your test was not conducted in accordance with the relevant regulations, although before doing this you are advised to seek legal advice.

List of DSA Regional Offices

DSA Head Office
Stanley House
Talbot Street
Nottingham
NG1 5GU
Tel: 0602-474222

DSA Regional Offices

Scotland
83 Princes Street
Edinburgh
EH2 2ER
Tel: 031-529-8595

North Eastern Region
Westgate House
Westgate Road
Newcastle-upon-Tyne
NE1 1TW
Tel: 091-201-4000

North Western Region
Portcullis House
Seymour Grove
Stretford
Manchester
M16 0NE
Tel: 061-876-4474

West Midlands Region
Cumberland House
200 Broad Street
Birmingham
B15 1TD
Tel: 021-608-1083

**Eastern Region
(Nottingham)**
Driving Test Bookings now at
Stanley House
Talbot Street
Nottingham
NG1 5GU
Tel: 0602-368206

**Eastern Region
(Cambridge)**
Terrington House
13-15 Hills Road
Cambridge
CB2 1NP
Tel: 0223-301100

Wales
Caradog House
1-6 St Andrews Place
Cardiff
CF1 3PW
Tel: 0222-373400
        0222-225186/7/8

Western Region
The Gaunts House
Denmark Street
Bristol
BS1 5DR
Tel: 0272-755121

South Eastern Region
Ivy House
3 Ivy Terrace
Eastbourne
BN21 4QT
Tel: 0323-417242

Metropolitan Region
PO Box 643
Charles House
375 Kensington High Street
London
W14 8TY
Tel: 071-605-0399
        (Guildford)
        071-605-0401
        (Croydon/
        Yeading)
        071-605-0408
        (Enfield/
        Purfleet)

Changes of Address for Correspondence including applications

All correspondence including applications for the following offices should be addressed to

Scotland
Westgate House
Westgate Road
Newcastle-upon-Tyne
NE1 1TW

**Eastern Region
(Nottingham & Cambridge)**
Stanley House
Talbot Street
Nottingham NG1 5GU

Western Region
Caradog House
1–6 St Andrews Place
Cardiff
Glamorgan CF1 3PW

All other DSA Regional Office addresses remain unchanged.

Driving Standards Agency Large Goods Vehicle (LGV) Driving Test Centres

Scotland

Aberdeen
Bishopbriggs (Glasgow)
Locharbriggs*
(Dumfrieshire)
Elgin (Keith)*
Galashiels*
Inverness
Kilmarnock
Kirkwall*
Lerwick*
Livingstone (Edinburgh)
Machrihanish (Kintyre)*
Oban*
Perth
Port Ellen*
Stornoway*
Wick*

North Eastern Region
Berwick*
Beverley
Darlington
Grimsby
Keighley
Leeds
Newcastle
Sheffield
Walton (York)

North Western Region
Bredbury (Stockport)
Carlisle
Heywood (Manchester)
Kirkham (Preston)
Simonswood (Liverpool)
Upton (Wirral)*

West Midlands Region
Garretts Green
(Birmingham)
Featherstone
(Wolverhampton)
Shrewsbury
Swynnerton (Stoke-on-Trent)

Eastern Region (Nottingham)
Alvaston (Derby)
Leicester
Watnall (Nottingham)
Weedon

Eastern Region (Cambridge)
Chelmsford
Ipswich
Leighton Buzzard
Norwich
Peterborough
Waterbeach (Cambridge)

Wales
Caernarvon*
Llantrisant
Llay (Wrexham)
Neath
Pontypool
Templeton (Haverfordwest)*

Western Region
Bristol
Cambourne
Chiseldon (Swindon)
Exeter
Gloucester
Poole
Plymouth
Taunton

South Eastern Region
Canterbury
Culham
Gillingham
Hastings
Isle of Wight*
Lancing
Reading
Southampton

Metropolitan Region
Croydon
Enfield
Guildford
Purfleet
Yeading

Note: * Tests are conducted only occasionally at these centres.

Other Useful Addresses

Driver and Vehicle Licensing Agency (DVLC) Swansea

DVLC
The Vocational Licence Section
Swansea
SA99 1BR

DVLC
Drivers Medical Branch
Swansea
SA99 1TU
Tel: 0792-304000

DVLC
Customer Enquiry Unit
Swansea
SA6 7JL
Tel: 0792-772151
Minicom: 0792 782787
Fax: 0792 783071
(Ring between 0815 and
16.30 Mon-Fri)

Part 4 Additional Information

City And Guilds of London Institute
46 Britannia Street
London
WC1X 9RG
Tel: 071-278-2468

Dept of Transport Enquiry Unit
2 Marsham Street
London
SW1P 3EB
Tel: 071-276-3000

Department of Transport Mobility Advice and Vehicle Information Service (MAVIS)
TRL
Crowthorne
Berkshire
RG11 6AU
Tel: 0344-770456

Freight Transport Association Limited
Hermes House
St John's Road
Tunbridge Wells
Kent
TN4 9UZ
Tel: 0892-526171

Health and Safety Executive Agency
See your telephone book for details of the area HSE office

Health and Safety Executive Agency
Enquiry Unit
Broad Lane
SHEFFIELD
Tel: 0742-892345

London Boroughs Transport Scheme (London Lorry Permit)
Night & Weekend lorry control scheme
The Secretary
Lorry Control Unit
Rooms 301-305 Hampton House
20 Albert Embankment
London SE1 7TJ
Tel:071-582-6220
Fax:071-582-1017

Road Haulage Association Limited (RHA)
Roadway House
35 Monument Hill
Weybridge
Surrey
Kent
KT13 8RN
Tel: 0932 841515

Road Haulage & Distribution Training Council Ltd.
Suite C
Shenley Hall
Rectory Lane
Shenley
Radlett
Herts WD7 9AN
Tel: 0923 858461
Fax: 0923 858491

Road Transport Industry Training and Business Services Ltd. (RSL)
MOTEC Telford
High Ercall
Telford TF6 6RB
Tel: 0952 770441
Fax: 0952 770926

RTITB Services Ltd (RSL)
11th Floor
York House
Empire Way
Wembley
Middlesex
HA9 0RT
Tel: 081-902-8880

Royal Society for the Prevention of Accidents (ROSPA)
22 Summer road
Acocks Green
Birmingham
B27 7UT
Tel: 021-706-8121

Part 4 Additional Information

Traffic Area Offices & Licensing Authorities

Scottish
83 Princes Street
Edinburgh
EH2 2ER
Tel: 031-255-5494

Area Covered: All Scotland & Islands

North Eastern
Hillcrest House
386 Harehills Lane
Leeds LS9 6NF
Tel: 0532-499433

Area Covered:
Northumberland
Tyne & Wear
Durham
Cleveland
Nottinghamshire
North Yorkshire
West Yorkshire
South Yorkshire
Humberside

North Western
Portcullis House
Seymour Grove
Stretford
Manchester
M16 0NE
Tel: 061-872-5077

Area Covered:
Cumbria
Lancashire
Merseyside
Greater Manchester
Cheshire

West Midlands
Cumberland House
200 Broad Street
Birmingham
B15 1TD
Tel: 021-631-3300

Area Covered:
Staffordshire
Shropshire
West Midlands
Hereford and
Worcester
Warwickshire

Eastern
Terrington House
13-15 Hills Road
Cambridge
CB2 1NP
Tel: 0223-358922

Area Covered:
Lincolnshire
Leicestershire
Northamptonshire
Buckinghamshire
Bedfordshire
Cambridgeshire
Norfolk
Suffolk
Essex
Hertfordshire

Wales
Caradog House
1-6 St Andrew's Place
Cardiff
CF1 3PW
Tel: 0222-394027

Area Covered:
Clwyd
Dyfed
Mid Glamorgan
South Glamorgan
West Glamorgan
Gwent
Gwynedd
Powys

Western
The Gaunt's House
Denmark Street
Bristol
BS1 5DR
Tel: 0272-755000

Area Covered:
Gloucestershire
Avon
Wiltshire
Somerset
Dorset
Devon
Cornwall
Oxfordshire
Berkshire
Hampshire
Isle of Wight

South Eastern and Metropolitan
Ivy House
3 Ivy Terrace
Eastbourne
BN21 4QT
Tel: 0323-721471

Area Covered:
West Sussex
East Sussex
Kent
Greater London
Surrey

Categories of Large Goods Vehicle Suitable for Test Purposes

Category	Description	Additional Categories Covered
C	A rigid goods vehicle with a maximum authorised mass of more than 7.5 tonnes not with automatic transmission	C with automatic transmissions
C with automatic transmission	As above but with automatic transmission	none
C+E	A rigid goods vehicle in category C drawing a trailer with more than one axle with a vehicle & trailer combination MAM of at least 15 tonnes not with automatic transmission. Or an articulated goods vehicle with a MAM of more than 7.5 tonnes, not with automatic transmission.	C+E with automatic transmission
C+E with automatic transmission	As above, but with automatic transmission	C with automatic transmission

MINIMUM TEST VEHICLES (Until 1st July 1996)

Category C	A lorry weighing more than 7,500kg
Category C+E	An articulated lorry or a rigid vehicle weighing more than 7,500kg with a trailer (total weight at least 15,000kg)

Vehicles used for a Large Goods Vehicle driving test must be UNLADEN

Note: Any signs, advertisements (other than on an original headboard, boxvan side or dropside), cones etc. constitute a 'burden'.

The vehicle effectively becomes LADEN and must therefore be taxed as a goods vehicle for which an operator's licence and insurance are required.

HGV Licences issued before 1 April 1991

There are SIX classes of heavy goods vehicle for HGV licence purposes, defined in the table below:-

Class	Definition	Additional classes covered
Class 1	An articulated vehicle, not fitted with automatic transmission (the tractive unit of which weighs more than 2 Tons)	Classes 1A, 2, 2A, 3 and 3A
Class 1A	An articulated vehicle, fitted with automatic transmission (the tractive unit of which weighs more than 2 Tons)	Classes 2A and 3A
Class 2	A heavy goods vehicle, not fitted with automatic transmission, other than an articulated vehicle designed and constructed to have more than four wheels in contact with the road surface	Classes 2A, 3 and 3A
Class 2A	A heavy goods vehicle, fitted with automatic transmission, other than an articulated vehicle, designed and constructed to have more than four wheels in contact with the road surface	Classes 3 and 3A
Class 3	A heavy goods vehicle, not fitted with automatic transmission, other than an articulated vehicle, designed and constructed to have not more than four wheels in contact with the road surface	Class 3A
Class 3A	A heavy goods vehicle, fitted with automatic transmission, other than an articulated vehicle, designed and constructed to have not more than four wheels in contact with the road surface	None

For the purposes of these definitions:

1 Where a vehicle is fitted with two wheels in line transversely and the distance between the centres of their respective areas of contact with the road is less than 18in, they are regarded as one wheel.

2 A vehicle with automatic transmission is defined as a vehicle in which the driver is not provided with any means whereby he may, independently of the use of the accelerator or the brakes, vary the proportion of the power being produced by the engine which is transmitted to the road wheels of the vehicle.

The Vocational Licence System 1 April 1991 onwards

On the new 'Community model' licence, driving entitlement is expressed in 'categories' as set out in the table below. Categories C, C plus E, D and D plus E are used for showing vocational entitlement.

Category	Description of vehicles included in the category
A	Motorbicycle (with or without sidecar) but excluding any vehicle included in category **K** or **P**
B	Motor vehicle with maximum authorised mass not exceeding 3.5 tonnes and not more than eight seats in addition to the driver's seat, not included in any other category and including such a vehicle drawing a trailer with a maximum authorised mass not exceeding 750Kg (Sub Cat. B1 7.5T + 750KG = 8.25T Max.)
B1	Motortricycle with a maximum design speed exceeding 50Km/h and an engine capacity greater than 50cc but excluding any vehicle included in category **K, L** or **P**
C	Motor vehicle used for the carriage of goods and whose permissible maximum weight exceeds 3.5 tonnes
C1	Motor vehicle used for the carriage of goods with a maximum authorised mass exceeding 3.5 tonnes but not exceeding 7.5 tonnes and including such a vehicle drawing a trailer with a maximum authorised mass not exceeding 750Kg (7.5T + 750Kg = 8.25T Max.)
D	Motor vehicle used for the carriage of passengers with more than eight seats in addition to the driver's seat
D1	Motor vehicle used for the carriage of passengers (but not for hire or reward) with more than eight seats, but not more than 16 seats, in addition to the driver's seat, and including such a vehicle drawing a trailer with a maximum authorised mass not exceeding 750Kg
B plus E	Combination of a motor vehicle in category **B** and a trailer with a maximum authorised mass exceeding 750Kg
C plus E	Combination of a motor vehicle in category **C** and a trailer with a maximum authorised mass exceeding 750Kg

The Vocational Licence System 1 April 1991 onwards

(Contd.)

C1 plus E	Combination of a motor vehicle in category **C1** and a trailer with a maximum authorised mass exceeding 750Kg
D plus E	Combination of a motor vehicle in category **D** and a trailer with a maximum authorised mass exceeding 750Kg
D1 plus E	Combination of a motor vehicle in category **D1** and a trailer with a maximum authorised mass exceeding 750Kg
F	Agricultural tractor, but excluding any vehicle included in category **H**
G	Road roller
H	Track-laying vehicle steered by its tracks
K	Mowing machine or pedestrian-controlled vehicle
L	Vehicle propelled by electric power but excluding any vehicle included in category **A**, **K** or **P**
N	Vehicle exempt from duty under section 7(1) of the Vehicle (Excise) Act 1971 (less than six miles on public roads per week)
P	Moped

On 1 April, 1991 holders of Class 3 or 3A licences (and restricted licences limiting the holder to driving vehicles which do not exceed 10 tonnes mpw) automatically became entitled to drive any rigid vehicles irrespective of the number of wheels on the vehicles.

Drawbar trailers may also be drawn in all cases.

For drivers who hold an HGV licence issued prior to 1 April, 1991 which has not yet been surrendered for a new unified licence, the entitlement to drive corresponding categories of large vehicles is as follows:-

Class of Heavy Goods Vehicle licence held	Categories of Large Goods Vehicle covered
1	B + E, C, C + E, D1, D1 + E
1A	as 1 but limited to vehicles with automatic transmission
2	B + E, C, C + E (limited to drawbar combinations only), D1, D1 + E
2A	as 2 but limited to vehicles with automatic transmission
3*	as 2
3A*	as 2A

* including licences restricted to 10 tonnes

Glossary of Terms

ABS Anti-lock braking system [developed by Bosch] which uses electronic sensors to detect when a wheel is about to lock, releases the brakes sufficiently to allow the wheel to revolve, then repeats the process in a very short space of time — thus avoiding skidding.

ADR Abbreviation used for European rules for the transport of hazardous materials by road.

Air Suspension System using a compressible material (usually air) contained in chambers located between the axle and the vehicle body to replace normal steel leaf spring suspension. Gives even load height (empty or laden) and added protection to fragile goods in transit.

Axle Weights Limits laid down for maximum permitted weights carried by each axle — depending on axle spacings and wheel/tyre arrangement (consult regulations, charts or publications giving legal requirements).

BS 5750 British Standards code relating to quality assurance adopted by vehicle body builders, recovery firms etc.

CAG Computer Aided Gearshift System developed by Scania which employs an electronic control unit combined with electropneumatic actuators and a mechanical gearbox. The clutch is still required to achieve the gear change using an electrical gear lever switch.

City of London Security Regulations Anti-terrorist measures mean that access to the City Of London is restricted to only seven access points involving closure of several other roads. Full details can be obtained from the Metropolitan Police.

CPC Certificate of Professional Competence indicates that the holder has attained the standards of knowledge required in order to exercise proper control of a transport business (required before an Operator's Licence can be granted).

C&U (Regs) Construction and Use Regulations specifications set out in law which govern the design and use of goods vehicles.

COSHH Regulations 1988 The Control of Substances Hazardous to Health Regulations 1988 place a responsibility on employers to make a proper assessment of the effects of the storage or use of any substances which may represent a risk to their employees' health. (details can be obtained from The Health & Safey Executive).

Cruise Control A facility which allows the vehicle to travel at a set speed without use of the accelerator pedal. However, the driver can immediately return to normal control by pressing the accelerator pedal.

Diff lock A device by which the driver can arrange for the drive to be transmitted to both wheels on an axle (normally rotating at different speeds when the vehicle is cornering, for example) which increases traction on surfaces such as mud, snow etc.

Double de-clutching Driving technique employed when driving LGVs which allows the driver to adjust the engine revs to the road speed when changing gear. The clutch pedal is released briefly while the gear lever is in the 'neutral' position. When changing down, engine revs are increased to match the engine speed to the lower gear in order to minimise the work load being placed on the synchro-mesh mechanism.

Important Note: The construction of modern gear boxes is such that this technique (improperly applied) can cause damage to the gearbox. In such instances, at least one major manufacturer has made it clear the warranty conditions will become invalid.

Drive-by-wire Modern electronic control systems which replace direct mechanical linkages.

Electronic engine management system The system monitors and controls both fuel supply to the engine and the contents of the exhaust gasses produced. The system is an essential part of some speed retarder systems.

Electronic Power Shift (Mercedes) semi-automatic transmission system requires the clutch to be fully depressed each time a gear change is made. The system then selects the appropriate gear.

Geartronic A fully-automated transmission system developed by Volvo. There is no clutch pedal. Instead, there is an additional pedal operating the exhaust brake.

GCW Gross combination weight applying to articulated vehicles.

GTW Gross train weight applying to drawbar combinations.

GVW Gross vehicle weight applying to solo rigid vehicles.

HSE Health & Safety Executive

Intermodal Operations Combined road and rail operations for the movement of goods where the 44 tonnes weight limit is authorised — subject to certain conditions.

Jake Brake (Jacobs Company) A long established system of speed retarding which alters the valve timing in the engine — in effect the engine becomes a compressor and holds back the vehicle's speed.

Kerb weight Total weight of a vehicle plus fuel excluding any load (or driver).

LA The Licensing Authority An official appointed to act on behalf of the Traffic Commissioners for a Traffic Area.

Lifting axle An axle which may be lowered or raised, depending on whether the load is required to be distributed to include the additional axle or the vehicle is running unladen. Such axles may be driven, steering or free-running.

Load sensing valve A valve in an air brake system which can be adjusted to reduce the possibility of wheels locking when the vehicle is unladen.

London Lorry Ban Night-time and weekend ban on lorries over 16.5 tonnes maximum gross weight applying to most roads in Greater London other than trunk roads and exempted roads. All vehicles other than special types or those concerned with safety or emergency operations must display a permit and exemption plate if they are to be used in the restricted areas. Note: Not **all** London boroughs still operate the scheme.

Part 4 Additional Information

LNG Liquified (Compressed) natural gas. (Also known as CNG).

LPG Liquified (Compressed) petroleum gas.

Plated Department of Transport regulations for recording and displaying information relating to dimensions and weights of goods vehicles indicating maximum gross weight, maximum axle weight and maximum train weight.

In the case of trailers the plate indicates maximum gross weight and maximum axleweight for each axle.

(This is in addition to any manufacturer's plate which is fixed to the vehicle or trailer)

Range Change Gearbox arrangement which permits the driver to select a series of either High or Low ratio gears depending on the load, speed and any gradient being negotiated. Effectively doubles the number of gears available (frequently up to a total of around 16 gears including crawler gears).

Red Routes Approximately 300 route miles in the London area are to become subject to stringent regulations restricting stopping, unloading and loading. (For details see Page 246).

Regrooving A process permitted for use on tyres for vehicles over an unladen weight of 2,540kg allowing a new tread pattern to be cut into the existing tyre surface (subject to certain conditions).

Retarder An additional braking system which may be

– mechanical as in the devices which either alter the engine exhaust gas flow or amend the valve timing (creating a 'compressor' effect)

– electrical where an electromagnetic field is energised around the transmission drive shaft (more frequently used on passenger vehicles).

SAMT Semi-automatic transmission system in which the clutch is only used when starting off or stopping.

Skip change Sequence of gear changing omitting intermediate gears sometimes known as selective gear changing.

Splitter Box Another name for a gearbox with High and Low ratios which effectively doubles the number of gears available.

Tacho Tachograph recorder indicating vehicle speeds, duration of journey, rest stops etc. required to be fitted to specified vehicles.

TBV Initials of French (Renault) semi-automatic transmission system employing a selector lever plus visual display information.

Thinking Gearbox Term used to describe fully automated gearbox which selects appropriate gear for load, gradient and speed etc. by means of electronic sensors.

Trailer swing occurs when severe braking causes partial loss of control as the rear wheels of a semi-trailer lock up on an articulated vehicle, or a draw-bar trailer becomes unstable.

Turbo (Charged) Forced air (fan driven) mixed with fuel to give increased engine performance.

Turbo (Cooled) Forced air (fan driven) in addition to liquid engine coolant system.

Two speed axle An electrical switch actuates a mechanism in the rear axle which doubles the number of ratios available to the driver.

Unloader valve Device fitted to air brake systems between the compressor and the storage reservoir preset to operate as sufficient pressure is achieved allowing the excess to be released (often heard at regular intervals when the engine is running).

VED Vehicle Excise Duty or Road Fund licence.

VRO Vehicle Registration Office dealing with matters relating to registration of goods vehicles, taxation and licensing.

Windscreen: Safety Glass
Toughened The glass receives a heat treatment process during manufacture so that, in the event of an impact (stone etc.) the screen breaks up into small blunt fragments reducing the risk of injury. An area in front of the driver is designed to give a zone of vision in the event of an impact.

Laminated A plastic film is sandwiched between two layers of glass so that an object, upon striking the screen, will normally indent the screen without large fragments of glass causing injury to the driver.

Wheel Arrangements

Identification of the ratio of the total number of wheels (excluding 'twin' wheels on one axle) compared with the number of wheels driven by the transmission system

Examples

4 x 2   Four wheels (2 axles): 2 driven wheels

6 x 2   Six wheels (3 axles): 2 driven wheels

6 x 4   Six wheels (3 axles): 4 driven wheels

6 x 6   Six wheels (3 axles): All wheels driven

8 x 4   Eight wheels (four axles): 4 driven wheels

LGV L-Plates

Either of the L plates shown in examples (a) and (b) can be displayed on vehicles used for vocational tests until 1 April 1996.

From that date, only the L plate shown in example (b) will be acceptable.

Example (a)

Example (b)

Hazardous Materials Labelling

Road Signs

Level crossing

Red Routes

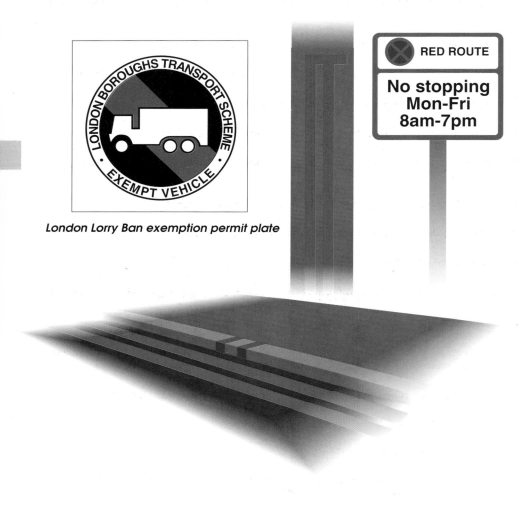

London Lorry Ban exemption permit plate

RED ROUTE

**No stopping
Mon-Fri
8am-7pm**

London Boroughs Transport Scheme
(London lorry permit)

Specimen Questions
Matters affecting safe control and operation of the vehicle

1. What safety factors are involved in stowage and loading of the vehicle?

2. What are some of the important reasons for ensuring a correct seating position?

3. What types of safety glass are used for windscreens?

4. What is the difference between laminated and toughened glass?

5. In an hydraulic braking system what does the necessity for pumping the pedal indicate?

6. What is a simple test for locating leaks in an air brake system?

7. Why does the vehicle dip forward when the brakes are applied?

8. What is 'brake fade'?

9. In frosty weather what could prevent air pressure building up in the brake reservoir?

10. With air brakes why is it particularly dangerous to coast downhill?

11. With an air brakes system, what is the usual visual safety aid to indicate insufficient compressed air in the storage tanks?

12. What other warning would indicate insufficient air in the storage tanks?

13. What is a two speed axle?

14. What is power-assisted steering?

15. If a power-assisted system fails, how will it affect the control of the vehicle?

Specimen Questions
Matters affecting safe control and operation of the vehicle
(contd.)

16. If you are aware of excessive emissions coming from the exhaust system of your vehicle —

    i. What does this tell you?

    ii. What should you do about it?

17. What action should you take if any brake low pressure warning device starts to operate?

18. What should you do if you discover an air or hydraulic leak in the braking system?

19. What safety checks should you make on your vehicle in relation to brakes, lights, steering and tyres, before starting a journey?

20. What important precaution must be taken before leaving any uncoupled trailer?

Specimen Questions
Uncoupling and re-coupling articulated vehicles

1. What factors should be taken into consideration in selecting a suitable place to leave an uncoupled semi-trailer?

2. What are the important factors in selecting a suitable surface for uncoupling?

3. In what order you would carry out the operations necessary to uncouple a semi-trailer from the tractive unit?

4. What should always be the first action before uncoupling?

5. What could be the result of failing to take this safety precaution?

6. When the semi-trailer landing gear has been lowered, what safety precaution should then be taken?

7. When uncoupling/re-coupling how should the tractive unit be driven?

8. On re-coupling what safety check should be made to ensure that tractive unit and trailer are securely coupled?

9. If the air line connections to the semi-trailer have self sealing valves, what special checks must be made?

10. How can you check that the trailer is receiving air from the tractive unit?

11. How should the landing gear be secured in the raised position?

12. Before reversing a tractive unit underneath a parked semi-trailer, what must you check first?

13. What is the correct order in which the re-coupling drill should be carried out?

14. Having re-coupled what is your last action before moving off?

Specimen Questions
Uncoupling and re-coupling vehicle & trailer combinations

1. What factors should be taken into consideration in selecting a suitable place to leave an uncoupled trailer?

2. What are the important factors in selecting a suitable surface for uncoupling?

3. Detail the order in which you would carry out the operations necessary to uncouple.

4. What should always be the first action in uncoupling?

5. What could result if you neglect to take this safety precaution?

6. When uncoupling/re-coupling how should the drawing vehicle be driven?

7. On re-coupling, what safety check should be made to ensure that the drawing vehicle and trailer are securely coupled?

8. If the air line connections to the trailer have self sealing valves, what special checks must be made?

9. How can you check that the trailer is receiving air from the drawing vehicle?

10. What check should be made to ensure that the brake lines and electrical leads are properly connected?

11. What is the correct order in which the re-coupling drill should be carried out?

12. How do you adjust the height of the drawbar to suit the drawing vehicle when coupling up?

Reversing exercise Cone position ready reckoner

LENGTH OF VEHICLE		CONE A	CONE B
METRES	FEET		
4.5	15	225	255
4.8	16	220	252
5.1	17	215	249
5.4	18	210	246
5.7	19	205	243
6.0	20	200	240
6.4	21	195	237
6.7	22	190	234
7.0	23	185	231
7.3	24	180	228
7.6	25	175	225
7.9	26	170	222
8.2	27	165	219
8.5	28	160	216
8.8	29	155	213
9.1	30	150	210
9.4	31	145	207
9.7	32	140	204
10.0	33	135	201
10.3	34	130	198
10.6	35	125	195
10.9	36	120	192
11.2	37	115	189
11.5	38	110	186
11.8	39	105	183
12.1	40	100	180
12.5	41	95	177
12.8	42	90	174
13.1	43	85	171
13.4	44	80	168
13.7	45	75	165
14.0	46	70	162
14.3	47	65	159
14.6	48	60	156
14.9	49	55	153
15.2	50	50	150
15.5	51	45	147
15.8	52	40	144
16.1	53	35	141
16.4	54	30	138
16.7	55	25	135
17.0	56	20	132
17.3	57	15	129
17.6	58	10	126
17.9	59	5	123
18.2	60	0	120

Part 4 Additional Information

Conclusion

We live in a world where vehicles and their loads can be tracked by satellite communication systems, where modern vehicles are fitted with 'smart engines' and 'thinking gearboxes', and where the driver is surrounded by all manner of electronic circuitry.

Today's large goods vehicle driver is no longer the grease-stained, grimy artisan figure clutching a shifting spanner.

Instead, he — or she — has to be a technician complying with all the legislation which governs the movement of goods on our roads.

Above all, you need to be a skilled dedicated driver and your driving should be to the highest standards.

It is in your own interests to keep up to date with changes in requirements as they occur. Ignorance is no defence in law.

Read the informative articles which appear in magazines devoted to driving large goods vehicles and remember that:

By passing the large goods vehicle driving test, you will be setting out on your career.

By studying this book you will have made your objective . . .

'Safe Driving for Life'

Mobile communications services · Fleet management · Vehicle tracking · Information technology · On-board computers

Printed in the United Kingdom for HMSO
Dd 296433 C100   2/94

The Index